STREETS PAVED
WITH GOLD

The Story of the

London City Mission

'The constantly-changing London scene has been changing more rapidly than ever in the twenty years since Phyllis Thompson was writing her history of the London City Mission, *To the Heart of the City*. In this new book, Irene Howat and John Nicholls have brought the story up to date with a wealth of documentation and historical and social background. I can vouch for part of their narrative personally, being myself an MK (missionary's kid!), and warmly commend this stirring tale of a great work of God in a great, needy, and challenging city.'

Michael Wilcock, Speaker and Author

'Reading this vivid account of the LCM we almost smell, hear and see the vibrant but tough areas where, down through the years, city missionaries have faithfully brought Jesus to the people of London. It is thrilling to see what God does through ordinary men and women filled with uncontrived godliness, dogged perseverance, true compassion and genuine friendliness. Irene and John, thank you for enlarging our vision of what God has done in London and can do in our own neighbourhoods too.'

John Ross, Greyfriars Free Church, Inverness

STREETS PAVED WITH GOLD

The Story of the London City Mission

Irene Howat and John Nicholls

Christian Focus and
London City Mission

ISBN 1-85792-781-8

© Copyright Christian Focus and London City Mission 2003

Published in 2003
by
Christian Focus Publications Ltd.
Geanies House, Fearn, Ross-shire,
IV20 1TW, Scotland
and
London City Mission, 175 Tower Bridge Road,
London, SE1 2AH

www.christianfocus.com

Printed and bound by
Cox & Wyman, Ltd. Reading, Berkshire

Cover Design by Alister MacInnes

Contents

Dedication

For Betty and Sarah

Acknowledgement

I wish to thank the London City Mission for the privilege of working on this history. It could not have been done without the help of missionaries, both active and retired, and their family members. Nor could it have been done without the consideration and patience of the staff of the Headquarters and Hostel.

Irene Howat

Foreword

The history of the London City Mission is remarkable for several reasons.

First, its dedication to *urban* mission was far ahead of its time. In the last few decades scholars have demonstrated how profoundly 'city-centric' early Christianity was. Paul ordinarily evangelized a region by going to its largest city (e.g. Acts 16:12.) Slowly the evangelical church has begun to recognize the importance of urban mission. But as we now turn our eyes to the city, we find the LCM already there! In some ways, we are just catching up to them.

Second, its unchanging devotion to the priority of evangelism is singular, almost unique. Innumerable denominations, colleges and schools, and other agencies have begun with the propagation of the gospel as their 'vision', only to lose it within one or two generations. The LCM, however, has doggedly kept the conversion of souls at the forefront of its institutional mission.

Third, its commitment to the poor, to immigrants – and to all other groups who could be called *'the least of these'* – is deeply impressive. People without power and respectability gravitate to the metropolis. There the LCM has welcomed them in Jesus' name.

How is it possible for such a large agency to have stayed so steadfastly committed to its vision for so long? The simplicity of its mission may be its 'secret.' *'The same person, going to the* same people, regularly, to become their friend, for Jesus' sake.' The LCM faces exciting but daunting new challenges in the 21st century. But despite the inevitable changes that will come, as it holds on to its core value of urban neighbour evangelism, it will continue to play a major, effective, strategic role in the work of the kingdom for the years to come. London is one of the three or four most influential urban centres in the world today. I am profoundly grateful that the London City Mission continues to be an anchor for gospel witness in that great city.

Tim Keller
Redeemer Presbyterian Church, New York City

Introduction

'Oh, London is a fine town,
A very famous city,
Where all the streets are paved with gold,
And all the maidens pretty.'
George Colman

'No, Sir, when a man is tired of London he is tired of life, for there is
in London all that life can afford.'
Samuel Johnson

'London, that great sea, whose ebb and flow
At once is deaf and loud, and on the shore
Vomits its wrecks, and still howls on for more.'
Percy Bysshe Shelley

'...this plague-house of sin and misery and corruption, where men
and women and little children starve and suffer and perish, body and
soul, is a sight to make one weep. We shall not wonder if some,
shuddering at the revolting spectacle, try to persuade themselves that
such things cannot be in Christian England...To such we can only
say, "Will you venture to come with us and see for yourselves the
ghastly reality?"'
Andrew Mearns, 'The Bitter Cry of Outcast London', 1883

The London City Mission has a long history, starting in the 19th century and still going strong at the beginning of the 21st. It began when Charles Dickens was writing *Oliver Twist*; and he might have been writing the first chapter of the LCM's story, so true to life was his description of the London of his day. It was against the backdrop of Fagin and Bill Sykes that the first City Missionaries began walking the far from golden streets of London, knocking on door after door, for week after week, till the years passed and the decades, and eventually the centuries.

The work of the London City Mission has developed in many different strands. To write the Mission's story starting at the beginning and working though to the present day would have presented a more complex tangle than a bowl of long spaghetti. We have, therefore, teased out areas of the LCM's work and told their stories one at a time.

The Mission has a fascinating archive, containing everything from the monthly Magazines and Annual Reports dating back to 1835, to handwritten and unpublished manuscripts penned by the missionaries themselves, together with a wealth of old lantern slides and photographs. Yet, apart from Phyllis Thompson's brief account marking the Mission's 150th anniversary, no overall survey of the LCM has appeared since the 1880s.

Although this history is written in words, we hope that it will conjure up pictures: of children like Oliver Twist; of women struggling to cope with grinding poverty; of London in two world wars; and of City Missionaries – men, and now women, who are still going door to door, on the streets of London, taking the message of God's salvation to all who live and work there. Long before anyone dreamt of London, a Hebrew king described that message as '*more precious than gold, than much*

pure gold'.   Through the work of the LCM many lives, if not
the very streets, have been 'paved with gold'.

Irene Howat and John Nicholls

1
Cholera

In 1849 *The Times* published a most unusual letter, signed by 54 Londoners. It read:

'*May we beg and beseech your proteckshion and power. We are Sur, as it may be, living in a Wilderniss, so far as the rest of London know anything of us, or as rich and great people care about. We live in muck and filthe. We aint got no privez, no dust bins, no drains, no water supplies, and no drain or suer in the whole place. ... The Stenche of the gully-hole is dusgustin. We al of us suffer, and numbers are ill, and if the Cholera comes Lord help us*' (quoted in *London, a Social History*, Roy Porter).

And the cholera did come, again and again. In 1849 there was a particularly virulent outbreak. In just one month in the late summer 10,000 Londoners died of the disease. The death toll was not spread evenly across the capital, but affected the poorer areas most severely. In one small area 81 adults died, together with 30 to 40 children. Some homes were hit harder than others:

'*A family consisting of 7 persons, the youngest a boy aged 14, not many doors from my own abode, were attacked* (by cholera), *and 5 died. The father, the boy of 14, and a daughter aged 16, were buried together at the same time, and the mother and a grown-up son in a day or two afterwards.*'

Cholera, although probably killing less people than typhus, was more feared because it was relatively new. First identified in India in 1818 (hence the common term 'Asiatic cholera'), it broke out in London for the first time in 1832. Medically, it was a bacterial stomach infection, which caused severe dehydration. Usually the first symptom of the disease was an attack of diarrhoea, although one victim wrote that for two or three days previously he had 'felt an indescribable weight and depression'. Continuing diarrhoea was accompanied by a severe fever, with 'cold, giddiness, nausea, vomiting and cramps'. In some cases death followed within a few hours of the first symptoms. In others, people lingered for two weeks before succumbing. Those who survived an attack were often left very weak for a lengthy period. Indeed, in 1855 a man who felt weak and ill traced his problem back to a severe bout of cholera in 1849.

We now know that cholera is a water-borne disease caused by sewage-polluted water, but in the 1840s the collective wisdom was that it was air-borne, with bad smells and a lack of fresh air being blamed for its virulence. A windmill was even built on top of the notorious Newgate Prison to prevent the air inside becoming stale and polluted. To protect Members of Parliament from 'The Great Stink' of the River Thames (which Disraeli once described as, *'a Stygian pool reeking with ineffable and unbearable horror')* the windows of the Palace of Westminster were lined with sheets of paper soaked in chlorine. In the poorer areas of London, housing was terribly overcrowded: in St. Giles district (near Tottenham Court Road) a typical house was described as follows:

'In the front room, a man and wife, and 9 children, 3 of whom were grown up, 2 men and their wives, and a single woman; total 16; two bedsteads. In the back closet, 2 men and their wives, and 2 single men, total 6; 2 bedsteads only,' 'Husband and wife and 4 children; husband and wife with 2 children; and 2 lads of 17 and 16, unconnected with the families, who pay for their bed between them, 1s

6d weekly.' 'Size of room, 12 feet long, 8 feet broad, 5 feet 6 inches high, occupied by one family and 3 widows; 1 male above 20; 4 females above 20, and 1 male under 20 ...'

As *The Times* correspondents had pointed out, such housing lacked any efficient sanitary arrangements. There was no clean water supply, and all kinds of sewage simply poured out into the streets and alleyways, where it lay in foul-smelling pools. In 1848 the Metropolitan Sanitary Commission had studied the situation and concluded that the wretchedness, filth, and brutal degradation they found was a disgrace to a civilised country. 'Improvements' in the form of splendid new buildings, such as those on New Oxford Street, only made matters worse. For those who had been rendered homeless by the demolition of what had been there before merely added to the overcrowding in the slums that remained elsewhere. The grand new buildings were not intended to house them!

Whenever cholera broke out, assuming that foul-smelling air was the problem, sanitary authorities embarked on a programme of flushing out the open cesspools. The immediate effect was a temporary relief of unpleasantness in the narrow streets, but the end result worsened the situation they set out to relieve. From the streets, the contents of the cesspools were flushed into the River Thames, only to be drawn out again as drinking and washing water, so doubly infecting those who used it.

In the summer of 1849 the disease took its course, instilling widespread fear. One man was so afraid of cholera that he left Westminster to stay with friends in Bristol. When he arrived he found that cholera was worse there than it was at home. He only remained one day before returning to Westminster. The night he arrived back he took ill and died the following day. In other households, well-to-do husbands forbade their charitably inclined wives to continue visiting the poor. While

city or shunned its reeking slums, there were
...d not. In Islington, for instance, a man not only
..district where cholera was rampant but also visited
...me where the disease had struck, doing whatever he
cou... to help, and recording each case in a detailed Journal.
The man was a London City Missionary, one of 201 who were
working in the metropolis' poorer areas when the epidemic
started. He provides graphic descriptions of some very human
victims:

*'Mrs — died of cholera on the 3rd..., after 38 hours' illness. She
was a member of the Wesleyan connexion, and although she did not
profess to have been converted, I believe she died a true Christian...*

*Mrs —, who lived at the corner of — Place, died of cholera on the
10th, after a few hours' illness. She was quarrelling very passionately,
and wishing the cholera might seize her own son at 11 o'clock at
night; but at 12 her wish fell upon herself, and the next evening she
was in eternity...*

*The next death is that of Mrs —, in the Almshouses, who died in the
90th year of her age. About 12 months ago she made a desperate
attempt at suicide....The last three months of her life were spent
principally in prayer...*

*The next case of death was that of a young woman who resided at
the cigar-shop. The last earthly enjoyment she had was at the fair,
held in the neighbourhood a week or two back; at the close of which
she was seized with cholera, of which she died on the 15th, in the most
desperate and malicious frame of mind imaginable.'*

The missionaries provided such medical advice and help as
they could. One wrote: *'In my visitations I have been in the habit
of carrying in my pocket opiate confection, and wherever I met with
any symptoms of the complaint at once gave a dose of it, all of whom
it relieved. I have been called out at ten, eleven, and twelve o'clock at
night and early in the morning. The only ill effects I have felt from it*

myself are that I have been so worn out as not to be able to sleep at night.'

This missionary was evidently following at least part of the medical treatment suggested by the Mission's Magazine:

'Twenty grains of opiate of confection, mixed with two table-spoonfuls of peppermint-water or a little weak brandy and water, and repeated every three or four hours, or oftener if the attack is severe, until the looseness of the bowels is stopped; or an ounce of the compound chalk mixture, with ten or fifteen grains of the aromatic confection, and from five to ten drops of laudanum, repeated in the same manner. From half a drachm to a drachm of tincture of catechu may be added to this last if the attack is severe...

When seized with cold, giddiness, nausea, vomiting, and cramps, get into a warm bed; use heated flannel, bags of hot camomile flowers, or heated bran, salt, or sand, or bottles of hot water, to produce warmth; have the extremities rubbed; apply a large poultice of mustard and vinegar over the region of the stomach, for fifteen or twenty minutes; drink every half-hour a spoonful of sal volatile in a little hot water, or a dessert-spoonful of brandy in a little hot water, or white wine whey (made by pouring one glass of sherry into a tumbler of hot milk): and send for the doctor as quickly as possible.'

City Missionaries also played a significant role in the long-term eradication of the disease. Their detailed reports on the true conditions in which so many people lived served to mobilise public opinion and politicians to investigate further the causes and prevention of cholera.

However, as the extracts from their Journals have shown, City Missionaries were concerned with more than health and housing. Their prime concern was for people's spiritual well-being. The Mission's 'Instructions to Agents' urged them to *'Visit the inhabitants of the District assigned to you for the purpose of bringing them to an acquaintance with salvation, through our Lord*

Jesus Christ, and of doing them good by every means in your power'. Even when they were bringing just a spoonful of opiate to a fever victim, they never lost their vision for the salvation of souls.

Beyond the awful reality of the cholera epidemic, these men saw another and greater evil hanging over the people of London. *'During the past month, there have been 10,000 deaths in London! Each day 333 immortal beings have been cut down, and received a sentence for eternity! How solemn a consideration! . . . Shall such a Society as the London City Mission witness the passing away of this fearful mass of men into an eternal world — so many of whom were cut off in a few hours, living in open sin to the day of their deaths — and Christian individuals be more remiss in seeking out for those bad districts which infect the moral well-being of the city, and more regardless to provide the means by which, through God's blessing, they may be spiritually cleansed, and future calamities so dreadful averted?* With its firm commitment to evangelical Christianity, the LCM viewed the people of London as spiritual beings, with souls as well as bodies, whose eternal destiny depended on their response to the Christian Gospel, and whose earthly lives would undoubtedly be transformed by a positive response. Unbelief and sin were seen as a 'spiritual cholera', affecting every single inhabitant of London, and bringing enslavement and death in this world and in the world to come.

At considerable cost to themselves, the missionary to Islington and his colleagues continued their pattern of visiting, helping, urging, and praying from room to room, throughout the 1849 epidemic. Many suffered bouts of cholera, and two died of the disease. Others saw it take members of their own families. But their work went on.

'From the time that the cholera became in any way alarming, depending on the mercy and goodness of God, and without conferring

18

*with flesh and blood, I determined on committing my life to Him who
is able to preserve it from evil, and set myself to be more than ordinarily
diligent on my district, in order that no one should die without being
visited and receiving spiritual instruction and consolation.'*

In the years that followed, cholera returned repeatedly to
London. But medical knowledge and technological skills were
developing. It was gradually realised that those areas which
drew their water from upstream of London had fewer cases of
cholera than those who used the polluted water at the city
centre. Under the direction of the new Metropolitan Board
of Works (forerunner of the London County Council), Joseph
Bazalgette began, in 1858, what a contemporary newspaper
called *'the most extensive and wonderful work of modern times'*
(*Observer*), the laying of 165 miles of main sewers and 1,100
miles of local sewers designed to disgorge their contents well
down-river of the metropolis. Reservoirs built to the north
and west of the city began to provide fresh water for its citizens.
And when, in the 1870s and 1880s, the embankments were
constructed, they altered the nature of the Thames,
transforming it from a wide and sluggish waterway to a
narrower, faster flowing, and altogether more healthy river
which, along with the city's sewage, eventually swept the
scourge of cholera away.

Historians have devoted much attention to the
transformation of London's health and sanitation in the 19th
century. But the story of the battle with 'spiritual cholera' is
not so well known. The men of the London City Mission
faced a greater and longer challenge than that overcome by
Bazalgette and his colleagues. They were by no means the
only Christians engaged in the battle, but they were, in
numerous ways, the vanguard of the great army of Victorian
evangelists and Christian social reformers. The story of the

origins, development and achievements of this 'London City Mission' deserves to be told.

2
Founding Fathers

'Few, save the poor, feel for the poor.'
Letitia Landor

'The object of this Institution is to extend the knowledge of the Gospel among the inhabitants of London and its vicinity (especially the poor), without any reference to denominational distinctions, or the peculiarities of Church Government.

To effect this object, Missionaries of approved character and qualifications, who shall give themselves entirely to the work, shall be employed and paid by the Institution...

...it is a fundamental law, that the following doctrines be prominently taught by the Agents and publications of the Mission..."All have sinned and come short of the glory of God." "In the beginning was the Word, and the Word was with God, and the Word was God. And the Word became flesh and dwelt among us." "Except a man be born again, he cannot see the kingdom of God." "The blood of Jesus Christ, God's Son, cleanseth us from all sin." "Being justified by faith, we have peace with God, through our Lord Jesus Christ." "Neither is there salvation in any other; for there is no other name under heaven given among men, whereby we must be saved." "Without holiness no man shall see the Lord." "Ye are sanctified – by the Spirit of our God."'
The LCM Constitution, May 1835

It was an unusual venue for a religious meeting, but the Music Hall in Store Street, just off the Tottenham Court Road, was so crowded that many people could not get in. Although the notorious slum district of St. Giles was just down the road, most of those at the meeting were from the respectable middle and upper classes. Among them was a sprinkling of Church of England clergymen and nonconformist ministers, an unusual occurrence at a time when arguments over the establishment of the Church were producing more heat than light among English Christians.

What had drawn such a mixture of people together on Monday 7th December 1835, was the first public meeting of the London City Mission. No less than 11 worthy men addressed the crowd, not to mention the reading of a lengthy Report on the first six months of the Mission's activity. No wonder the Chairman felt it necessary to give a detailed summing up before the meeting closed with a hymn and a prayer! The collection that evening amounted to £94 17s (in a day when a missionary's annual salary was about £60) and more gifts were handed in at the close. When the LCM Committee met the following day they were told of other exciting results: a leading minister had indicated his willingness to preach a sermon in support of the Mission, and specific pledges of funding had been made so that missionaries could be placed at Broad Street (in the oldest part of London, known as 'The City') and at Islington. In fact, so much money had been raised that it was agreed to advertise for 20 new missionaries to join the ten who were already at work – an increase of 200 per cent. The Committee ordered that 2,000 extra copies of the Report be printed, together with 1,000 copies of the speeches made at the meeting. London City Mission was well and truly in business!

Six months previously, the prospects had looked far less healthy. The Mission had not exactly started with a bang. It took three attempts to arrange the founding business meeting, and even then it saw just three laymen gathering in a small terraced cottage by the banks of the Regents Canal in unfashionable Hoxton. There, on 16th May 1835, they formed themselves into the London City Mission, and agreed on a detailed statement of the organisation's aims and methods. But it is one thing to found a ministry on paper, quite another to have it widely accepted and generously funded. What was it that drew such crowds to Store Street less than seven months later? What made the first public meeting so successful?

The first reason for the LCM's dramatic progress was embodied in the man who chaired the Music Hall meeting, a man who was soon to be referred to as 'The Father of the Mission'. The Honorable and Reverend Baptist Wriothesley Noel not only had a remarkable name, he also had a remarkable ministry. The younger brother of the Earl of Gainsborough, he had all the status and wealth of a member of the aristocracy. An ordained clergyman of the Church of England from 1823, twenty-five years later he would shock the Church by leaving and becoming a nonconformist. But in 1835, he was minister of St. John's Chapel in Bedford Row, the main rallying point for evangelical Anglicans in London, and was famous because he had just published an open letter, addressed to the Bishop of London, on the spiritual and moral destitution of the city.

The overgrown monster

Baptist Noel's letter surveyed the religious situation of a city that was experiencing staggering growth as the Industrial Revolution gripped Britain. In 1801, London's population was still below one million. A hundred years later it would be over

23

6.5 million. In the first four decades of the 19th century the population virtually doubled, a phenomenon no one had ever before experienced. Back in the 1720s, Daniel Defoe had considered London *'an overgrown monster'*. By the 1830s *'confidence in London hit a low; its problems of growth — crime, destitution, epidemic disease, overcrowding — seemed to be on the verge of overwhelming the city'* (Peter Hall, *Cities in Civilization*). As we have seen, the poor lived in appalling conditions, in ruinous houses, largely destitute of furniture and totally without clean water and proper sanitation. The streets were filthy beyond description; they were, in fact, just open sewers. It was little wonder that health deteriorated, infectious diseases spread and the death rate was high. *The Times* pontificated that *'a great town is a great evil'* (ibid), and that certainly seemed to be the case in London.

Today most people know that London in the early 19th century spawned much human suffering and social evil. But in 1835 Charles Dickens was largely unknown and much of the country, including many well-to-do Londoners, lived in total ignorance of what life was like in the world of the slums and rookeries. It was this world that Baptist Noel described in his letter to the Bishop, but (unlike Dickens) he considered that the problem was spiritual as well as physical and social.

'There is something, my Lord, unspeakably painful, in the contemplation of this mass of immortal beings ..., living, as we have reason to fear, without God and without hope,' began Baptist Noel's letter, before going on to outline the problem as he saw it. *'...500,000 Sabbath-breakers at the very least, in total neglect of the restraints of religion — 10,000 of these are devoted to play, about 20,000 are addicted to beggary, 30,000 are living by theft and fraud, 23,000 are annually picked up drunk in the streets, about 100,000 are habitual gin-drinkers, and, probably, 100,000 have yielded*

themselves to systematic and abandoned profligacy.' Noel's letter led to much discussion of what the church should be doing. The problem of the impoverished masses was on the public agenda. Noel was not only a man of well-chosen words; he was also a man of action. Deeply committed to co-operating with Christians from other denominations, he had already started a regular gathering of some 15 ministers – from the Established Church and nonconformists – for prayer and sharing about the best ways to reach the poor with the Christian gospel. One of this group was a young Church of Scotland minister named John M'Donald, who preached both in his Islington church and also in the open air, where up to 500 people gathered to hear him. But such efforts by a handful of men revealed the need for a much larger ministry. So it was that Baptist Noel prepared the way for the London City Mission. For him, it seemed only natural to give the new organisation his full support. A few years later, another London minister addressed Noel in the following terms: '... *you boldly appeared on the platform, at the first Public Meeting held on behalf of the infant Mission, and so conferred on it the benefit of your rank, reputation, and eloquence ... You did more than any other man of your class – more, indeed, than all of them united – to assist in founding and establishing the London City Mission*' (John Campbell, *Memoirs of David Nasmith*) .

While Baptist Noel chaired the Store Street meeting, the first speaker he introduced was the actual founder of the LCM. His name was David Nasmith, and he had arrived in London just as Noel published his letter to the Bishop. Nasmith already had a remarkable record of achievement, even though he was just 36 years old, and had a burning passion to get to grips with what he saw as the spiritual and social needs of his day. He was a compulsive founder of societies. Beginning in his native Glasgow, he had travelled throughout Ireland, America, Canada and France – in a day when travel was far from easy and journeys very long – contacting ministers and other Christians in about 250 cities, towns and villages, persuading them to organise themselves into City Missions, Young Men's Societies, Tract Societies, Adult School Societies, and Societies to provide Refuges for Fallen Women. He well deserves his place in Geoffrey Hanks' book *60 Great Founders*!

The influence of Thomas Chalmers

Over the years, Nasmith had developed a blueprint for City Missions, building on the pioneering urban ministry of Thomas Chalmers in Glasgow from 1815 to 1820. Chalmers had divided his vast overcrowded parish into small districts, each with a population of just a few hundred people. To each district volunteer visitors were assigned with instructions to go from door to door getting to know the inhabitants. Having built up some degree of local knowledge and trust, the visitors were to organise Sunday Schools, help people find work, and take the Christian gospel to those who would never go to church to hear it for themselves. This basic system was widely copied throughout Britain in the 1820s and 1830s, with volunteer District Visitation Societies springing up in many towns and cities. But Nasmith developed it significantly. For one thing, he separated the programme of visitation from the provision of any kind of official financial relief for the poor, Chalmers having been heavily involved in Poor Law reform. For another, he founded his missions on an interdenominational basis, asserting that the scale of the urban problem was so great that Christians could only hope to make an impact if they set aside differences about church government and got on with the job together. Finally, Nasmith recognised the inadequacy of the volunteer system and took the remarkably bold decision to recruit and pay full-time, non-ordained workers to do the work of evangelistic visitation. These workers, unlike most of the volunteers, were men and came mainly from the working classes.

This, then, was the blueprint David Nasmith brought to London in 1835, having already put it into action in other countries. At the Store Street meeting, one of the speakers was an American minister, Mr J.O. Choules, who *'could bear a cheerful testimony to the labours and fidelity of Mr Nasmith, so far as America was concerned'* (Jan. 1836). The Scot had tirelessly walked the streets of London, seeking interviews with clergy and laymen, advocating his scheme. Not that he had been immune from discouragement – even Baptist Noel at first doubted whether an interdenominational society could possibly be founded in the religious politics of the time – but Nasmith would not be deterred. Noel, when he decided on the rightness of co-operation, was not shy of sharing his views. *'Perhaps it may linger in the minds of some ... that we should not all unite in this great work ...(But) if we did not all unite we could not find the men that are fitted for this work, and that should reach the wants of this population; all must be combined ... So long as those who have the charge of this Institution have their eyes fixed on the main object to be attained – so long as they forget all that sectarian feeling, and all bitterness of mind, which interfere with a true brotherly spirit, and a zeal for the cause of the Redeemer ... the association can only lead to the most inestimable results.'*

We can only imagine what Nasmith must have felt in December 1835 as he gazed out from the platform at that crowded meeting. Things had come a long way from the cottage in Hoxton, and in just a few months! He said that Baptist Noel's letter to the Bishop had unmistakeably shown the *need* for such a mission. Now they must overcome the difficulties and obey the command of the Lord Jesus Christ, 'Go out *quickly* into the streets and lanes of the city, and bring in hither the *poor*.'

David Nasmith's scheme, relying as it did on paid workers, required considerable financial support. In 1835, he envisaged a team of 400 missionaries, visiting all the needy areas of London. That would require about £25,000 a year for men's salaries alone! Today, we are very familiar with fund-raisers, high-profile advertising, and tear-jerking television appeals for the relief of disasters and other worthy causes, but in those days there were more limited means available.

Anti-slavery campaigner

If Noel had prepared the ground for the City Mission and Nasmith had provided the plan and the spark, the contribution of a third man was also essential to the success of the Store Street meeting, even though it does not seem that he was there! Thomas Fowell Buxton was, in 1835, one of the most famous men in England. The owner of a large brewery in Brick Lane, he had a deep concern for the spiritual and social needs of London's poor. However, it was not in the brewery that he had made his name, but in the corridors of the Palace of Westminster. When he became a Member of Parliament in 1819, he immediately joined William Wilberforce in the campaign against slavery. Wilberforce had persuaded Parliament to outlaw the British trade in slaves in 1807, but slavery itself remained legal in British colonies and the fight for the emancipation of all slaves continued. When frailty overtook Wilberforce, Buxton assumed the leadership of the cause and eventually won the great battle against the vested interests of the slave owners and their financial backers. In

1833 the Act of Emancipation was passed, and on 1st August 1834 all slaves in British dominions were officially free.

A year later, when Nasmith wrote inviting him to become Treasurer of the new London City Mission, Thomas Buxton was at the height of his fame and influence, with free access to the Prime Minister and members of the government. Although he continued to champion the cause of the oppressed in Africa and elsewhere, Buxton readily agreed. Thus began a lengthy association between the Buxton family and the LCM that lasted until after World War I. Thomas Buxton not only had personal experience of the needs of London's poor, he was also married to one of the famous Gurney family of Quakers, and thus a brother-in-law of Elizabeth Fry, the prison reformer. For the infant City Mission, Buxton's name meant instant recognition and respect. After all, the society's Treasurer had presented massive petitions to Parliament on the slavery issue; he had mobilised British evangelicals to support the crusade, and he had succeeded in bringing about peaceful emancipation when many had warned of bloodshed and revolution in the colonies. With Thomas Buxton's name appearing on all the LCM's reports and financial appeals, the society could confidently expect wide support from across the country. Along with Baptist Noel and David Nasmith, Thomas Fowell Buxton well merits the title Founding Father of the London City Mission.

3

Acceptance

'There has been much affliction during the year and many who during the affliction promised to seek the Lord have with returning health, forgotten their promises and continue to go in sin but I am thankful to report that there are two cases in which there is evidence to show the affliction has been made the means of conversion. The first, Mr Peachey.   He and his wife always received me with civility but I could not prevail on him to attend the house of God but in August he was visited with severe affliction.   I was sent for to visit him and I found him acknowledging himself a sinner.   I endeavoured to press this home upon his conscience and urged him to fly to Jesus Christ for refuge.   After a few visits I thought he began to feel deeply on this subject.   He was brought very low so that he was not expected to survive many hours but he recovered. As soon as this was the case he showed that he had derived benefit from his affliction by making the Bible his frequent companion and by attending with his wife at the house of God. They are both determined to serve God and say they find his ways to be pleasantness and peace.'

Annual Report of William Hurling, missionary in Haggerstone 1843

'We are happy to state that the Committee have engaged the services of a missionary to soldiers, who will, during the month of August, D.V., commence his special work. He himself served in the army 23½ years as a private soldier, corporal, schoolmaster, paymaster-sergeant, quarter-master-sergeant, and staff-sergeant-Major.'

The LCM Magazine, Aug. 1848

Instructions to Missionaries

1. Visit the inhabitants of the District assigned to you for the purpose of bringing them to an acquaintance with salvation, through our Lord Jesus Christ, and of doing them good by every means in your power.

2. Read a portion of the Word of God in every house, if you have an opportunity; when this cannot be done, introduce into your conversation as much of the Scriptures as possible, and see that the terms used are understood. In reading or speaking, let those portions of Scripture that bear on the depravity of man and the way of salvation through faith in Christ alone, ever hold a prominent place...

4. Urge upon every one, the duty of attending the public worship of God. If they attend no place of worship, direct them to those places in the locality in which the Gospel is preached; and beware, directly or indirectly, of seeking to promote the interests of a party; the sole object of the Mission being to bring sinners to the Saviour...

13. Conduct yourself in such a manner as will prove to all persons that you are in earnest in seeking their spiritual welfare. Be humble, courteous, and affectionate. Constantly realise your own obligations to the Saviour. Go to your District in a spirit of prayer, and with an earnest desire that every person you visit may be brought to a saving knowledge of the Lord Jesus Christ. Your work is awfully important; you have to deal with immortal souls, many of whom may never hear the Gospel but from you, and whose eternal condition may be determined by the reception or rejection of the message which you deliver to them. Be courageous, be faithful, keep the Lord Jesus Christ continually before your own mind, and commend Him and his great salvation to the people...

Let the glory of God and the salvation of souls be your chief, your only end.

The Annual Meeting of the London City Mission in May 1848 was held in exciting and anxious times. Revolution was sweeping Europe. In Paris, Berlin and Vienna that Spring had seen violent uprisings, mass shootings and other such horrors. It seemed that the dark days of the French Revolution, the Terror, were likely to return, and that they might cross the English Channel and reach London. On 6th March a crowd of some 10,000 protesters seized Trafalgar Square, for two days defying police to evict them. The Chartist movement planned a vast demonstration at Kennington Common on April 10th, to be followed by a march to Parliament bearing a petition signed by 5 million people demanding reform. Fearing revolution, the government called in 8,000 troops and 1,000 retired soldiers to support the capital's 4,000 police. In the event, however, the great demonstration turned out to be a damp squib. Although as many as 100,000 may have gathered at Kennington, there was no march to Westminster and no revolution.

Lord Kinnaird, who was accompanied on to the platform by an Earl and two Members of Parliament, chaired the LCM meeting just a month later. In his opening speech, he said, '*It is my firm belief, that in the late confusion and difficulty which seemed to hang over this metropolis, the agency of the London City Mission, along with other bodies of a like character, did most materially contribute to keep the whole metropolis at peace. Large masses of the community have learned that they really are cared for, and that there are persons who make it their constant and unceasing business to consider their temporal and eternal welfare. I do not believe that ten years ago this town could have withstood the mighty shock that came from the continent.*' Certainly the Mission was reaching the people who were most likely to resort to violence. The missionary who visited a notoriously crowded and impoverished area called

Plumtree Court reported that when he went there on 10th April, he found it '*as a depopulated village. Its entire population was cleared out to march in procession to Kennington-common.*'

The view that the LCM had been a major contributor to peace was shared by Lord Ashley. *(Anthony Ashley Cooper [1801– 1885] was known as Lord Ashley until 1851 when he became the seventh Earl of Shaftesbury. For the sake of simplicity he will be referred to as Shaftesbury from now on.)* Then, and for years afterwards, he was heard to insist that London's escape from the bloodshed and chaos of 1848 was, at least in part, due to the patient ministry of the missionaries of the LCM among the very poorest parts of the population. And remarks like that were heard and noted in Europe. The French statesman M. Guizot, who knew better than most the havoc revolution brought in its wake, told Shaftesbury that, '*The religion alone of your country has saved you from revolution.*' In Sweden, the king and queen were sufficiently impressed to give a donation to a new City Mission founded in Stockholm, in the hope that it would bring similar benefits there.

0 to 197 in 13 years!

Such public acclaim underlined the achievement of the teenaged Mission. And how it had grown! By 1848 there were 197 missionaries working in districts from Barnet in the north to Peckham, Sydenham and Richmond in the south. There were also four specialist missionaries working with the police, cabmen, and the city's Italian population. In the short lifetime of the LCM, City and Town Missions had been founded across the country, and missions in direct imitation of London's had been founded in places as different and as distant as Madras and Barbados. But the LCM was not in a mood to rest on its laurels. The income from 1847 having been in excess of

£16,000, there were bold plans for further expansion. That was only possible because in its first 13 years the society had become part of the religious and social scene. By 1848, its Committee included Members of Parliament, Lords and many well-known names.

Growing pains

Not that this status had been achieved easily or smoothly. Far from it. The worst crisis had been the earliest, and it almost destroyed the young Mission when it was not two years old. The root problem was the chronic suspicion and hostility that marred relations between the established Anglican Church of England and the nonconformist denominations. From the beginning, many Anglicans (including some evangelicals) had refused to have anything to do with the Mission. Because it was not under the authority of the Bishop of London, and its missionaries often worked independently of parish ministers, they regarded it as something of a nonconformist Trojan horse. The Bishop himself at one time tried to ban all his clergy from involvement in the Mission's work. As a result, several Anglicans resigned from the Committee and others withdrew from examining the LCM's recruits. But not all capitulated. Some took a firm stand, and the Bishop eventually relented.

This crisis caused one notable casualty – none other than the Mission's instigator, David Nasmith. Faced with Anglican suspicions and their dwindling support, the Committee proposed a change in the constitution, guaranteeing equal representation of Anglicans and nonconformists on both the Committee and list of examiners. Nasmith baulked at this, insisting that it would be wrong to thus formalise denominational divisions. He argued that Christians zealous for evangelism should be above such pettiness. While his idealism was doubtless attractive, the Committee (no less zealous for evangelism) was more realistic. They won the day. David Nasmith, whose conscience would not allow him to work within the new set-up, insisted on resigning, just 21 months after the Mission began. Perhaps, however, his departure was a necessary step in the progress of the Mission, for he seems to have had the characteristics of a rugged pioneer, which do not always sit comfortably with the long-term smooth running and development of a large organisation.

When Nasmith died suddenly, just two years later, the Mission's Committee was fulsome in its gratitude for him. '*In reviewing his short career in London and England, they feel devoutly thankful to Almighty God for the great blessings conferred through his instrumentality upon London in particular, and upon other cities and towns in Britain: many Institutions having been formed by him, or having originated in his labours, calculated to be of lasting benefit to future generations, especially the adoption, and carrying out of the great principle of City Missions by the united labours of Evangelical Christians of different denominations ... no eulogy of the deceased would be so harmonious with his feeling could he now read it, as their solemn determination to tread in those steps which will lead to a larger diffusion of the Gospel of Christ ...*' The LCM placed a memorial stone in Bunhill Fields, where he was buried. Later, when Bunhill Fields closed for health reasons, another stone was erected in Highgate Cemetery.

David Nasmith was succeeded at the centre of the Mission's management by the Rev. John Garwood, formerly the vicar of St. Mary's Spitalfields, and a man with the courage to face down his hostile Bishop. He was to continue as the London City Mission's Secretary for nearly 40 years, and to him is due much of the credit for consolidating and developing what Nasmith had initiated.

Early effectiveness

In its early years the LCM engaged in several high-profile campaigns, some of which achieved their goal; but all helped the Mission gain public recognition and support. These included the distribution of 36,000 New Testaments to homes that had been found to be without any Scriptures. There were also campaigns against the Fairs held at Smithfield, Hainault and elsewhere, which had become notorious for prostitution, drunkenness and crime. As a result of the LCM publicity and appeals to national and local government, these events were either curtailed or abolished. While the events in the murky world of ecclesiastical politics saved the Mission from an early demise, and public campaigns made it well known, its positive acceptance and on-going support derived mainly from the quality and effectiveness of the work of individual missionaries in their districts. It was because their work really made a difference, and was seen to make a difference, that the LCM achieved the stability it had by 1848.

Under Nasmith's scheme, when suitable men were selected they were appointed to clearly defined districts, each with a population of a few thousand people. They were to work only in their own districts, and their basic task was to go to the people with the gospel. So they went from house to house and door to door, introducing themselves, listening to what people had to say – and it was often harrowing stories they heard – talking when given the opportunity, trying to persuade people to read the Bible, go to church and send their children to Sunday School. Because they met people in their home situations, and often heard the sad details of their lives, they inevitably and willingly became concerned about, and involved in, their district's social and practical problems. Although forbidden to hand out money, they were able to report cases of need and hardship to wealthy Christian friends who might have it in their hearts to help. Missionaries' days ended with writing their Journals; these were provided by Headquarters and inspected on a regular basis. Their Journals and Annual Reports, along with information they were able to convey, became an important and almost unique source of information on the true conditions of the poorest areas of London. In days before the advent of social workers, compulsory education, a state health service, or a large-scale police force, the City Missionaries were virtually the first professionals to go systematically through the streets and homes of London, keeping careful records and writing regular reports on all aspects of life. Committees of Parliament and local and national social reformers looked to them for statistics and for opportunities to see the worst areas for themselves. One of the first books published by the Mission was sub-titled, 'One half of London's population introduced to the other half'. The missionaries' role as information gatherers was of great significance.

Our man in Clerkenwell

Typical of such early district visitation was that of Robert Vanderkiste, who wrote of the Cowcross District, in Clerkenwell, as it was in 1845. *'The state and character of the inhabitants of various portions of the district almost baffle description. Extreme ignorance and extreme drunkenness prevail. The children grow up hardened and vicious. Half-starved and half-naked, the boys crowd in shoals, meditating plunder. Fights are common, amongst women as well as men. The dirtiness of the habits of the people in many instances is extremely repulsive; this arises partly from their extreme poverty and partly from drunkenness. When I was first appointed to the district I was seized with violent itchings between the joints, accompanied with* redness. *Bugs and fleas and other vermin abound. I have to examine my clothes carefully each day, and while visiting at night have sometimes seen numbers of bugs coursing over my clothes and hat, and have had much trouble to get rid of them. The stenches, also, have sometimes been so bad that my mouth has filled with water, and I have been compelled to retreat.*' He told of poor women who took to their beds, not because they were ill, but because they had washed their only clothes and had nothing to wear while they were drying; of a gypsy boy whose only clothing was an old sack fastened at the waist; and of the pathetic occupations by which many barely scratched a living – including collecting the dog dung that was used in the production of morocco leather.

In such an environment, Vanderkiste visited regularly from room to room, gradually gaining acceptance in courts and houses where the police dared not go. He did what he could to arrange for the provision of clothes for the near naked and food for the hungry, but he also addressed one of the root causes of poverty – the total lack of education of many in his district – by starting Ragged Schools for both children and adults. Within a few years, some 300 children were attending the day school. A further 186 older children and adults attended the evening school, many coming straight from a day's work that had started at dawn or before. A Sunday evening service was begun, and was well attended.

Missionaries did not gain acceptance either automatically or easily. Years later, one looked back to his first day on a new district and remembered the time and effort acceptance cost. '*I had not been many hours at work when the report spread that I was a policeman in disguise, and I was hounded out of the place by a desperate, howling mob of thieves and outcasts. Upon my return home I was so cast down as only to be able to gain relief in tears and prayer. Next day I went very cautiously to work; but upon ascending a very steep, rickety staircase, a woman with*

39

hobnail boots came onto the landing, and with bitter oaths declared 'if I came a step higher that she would kick my eyes out'; so I had to beat a retreat. This desperate effort to gain footing in the place continued for several months ... This perseverance, however, with the word of the living God, was effective, and constant, brutal oppression was overcome, though for long years I was subjected to low abuse and occasional acts of violence. After several years I gained entrance into many rooms and into most of the dens. My care for the sick and the children disarmed opposition, and then in room after room attention was secured to the readings of the Bible. A few began attending the little meeting I had established. A few years more and a real friendship was entertained for me by most unlikely people. The Ragged School I had established was crowded with children, and my meeting was increasingly well attended. Soul after soul was brought under conviction, and many were gathered into the fold of Christ. The neighbourhood was indeed opened up to the clergy, ministers, and a few lay workers ...'

The Magazine

Such reports were regularly published in the London City Mission Magazine, which was first produced in January 1836 and appeared monthly thereafter. Sometimes articles in the Magazine offended local clergy because they were stung by suggestions that they did not visit their parishes as diligently as they might. Occasional apologies and clarifications were published to smooth ruffled feathers. The Mission was very careful to check, so far as it could, that reports and the claims they made were accurate. In 1848, a missionary in Hackney was summarily dismissed when it was found that he had falsely claimed to have successfully encouraged people to become church members.

In this and other ways, great care was taken to see that missionaries maintained the standards and ideals of the society. Recruitment was a thorough process, fewer than half of the applicants being accepted. In addition to those rejected because they lacked the necessary qualities of Christian knowledge, one man, 'J.B.' was *declined, being in the judgment of the managers unfit for the work, from the high opinion he expressed of his own capability'*. Cases of misconduct (there were a few) were dealt with firmly by the Committee as soon as they came to light.

Some missionaries stayed with the LCM for a few years then left. Others became ill and had to leave, and several died of diseases caught in the course of their work. But a good number spent decade after decade working in the unappealing conditions of the London slums, earning the respect of the people in their districts and the admiration of the London City Mission's growing band of supporters. The LCM had become an accepted and influential part of the growing evangelical attack on the perceived social, moral and religious evils of early Victorian London.

4

Ragged Schools

'*While beholding these poor little creatures, whose delicate limbs are scarcely clothed with rags, you think you see flowers covered with mud!*'
(Les Ecoles en Haillons, 1850).

LCM   Questions to Candidates

1. Have you reason to think that you are a partaker of Divine grace, and on what grounds do you arrive at that conclusion?

2. What are your views of the leading doctrines of Christianity?

3. What are your views respecting the qualifications necessary for the work of the London City Mission?

4. Have you been engaged in the instruction of the young, in seeking the spiritual benefit of the sick, in visiting the poor, in the distribution of tracts? In what other ways have you endeavoured to render yourself useful?

N.B. Spiritual-mindedness, and a facility in referring to texts of Scripture in proof of the various doctrines and duties taught and enjoined in the Word of God, are deemed essential and indispensable qualifications.

'London is a city of 3 million inhabitants and they are mostly fools.'
Thomas Carlyle

'A gentleman ... was engaged in earnest conversation with one of our District Secretaries. "Ah!" he said, "I owe much to the London City Mission. Many years ago, when I was a child in a Ragged School, it was a City Missionary who taught me the first prayer I ever uttered; and to-day I am worth £20,000!" Such an instance is, of course, exceptional.'
The LCM Magazine, Dec. 1883

As the men of the young London City Mission tramped the streets and alleyways of their districts, they met the conditions described by Dickens. '*Covent-garden Market, when it was market morning, was wonderful company. The great wagons of cabbages, with growers' men and boys lying asleep under them, and with sharp dogs from market-garden neighbourhoods looking after the whole, were as good as a party. But one of the worst sights I know in London, is to be found in the children who prowl about this place; who sleep in the baskets, fight for the offal, dart at any object they think they can lay their thieving hands on, dive under the carts and barrows, dodge the constables, and are perpetually making a blunt pattering on the pavement of the Piazza with the rain of their naked feet. A painful and unnatural result comes of the comparison one is forced to institute between the growth of corruption as displayed in the so much improved and cared for fruits of the earth, and the growth of corruption as displayed in these all uncared for (except inasmuch as ever-hunted) savages*' (*Oliver Twist*).

Dickens' description is verified by no less than the Earl of Shaftesbury, who wrote in the *Quarterly Review*, that he found children, '*in squalid and half-naked groups at the entrances of narrow fetid courts and alleys ... The foul and dismal passages are thronged with children of both sexes, and of every age from three to thirteen. Though wan and haggard, they are singularly vivacious, and engaged in every sort of occupation but that which would be beneficial to themselves and creditable to the neighbourhood. Their appearance is wild; matted hair, disgusting filth, barbarian freedom from all restraint ... Visit these regions in summer and you are overwhelmed by the exhalations; visit them in winter and you are shocked by the spectacle of hundreds shivering ... all but naked.*'

These same children scuttled around the feet of the City Missionaries, and tugged at their heart-strings. On 18th May 1840, at the Mission's Annual Meeting in the Exeter Hall, one of the topics was what was being done for them. By then, several missionaries had opened schools, five of the establishments being specifically for children 'raggedly clothed'. These five were in Lambeth, Rosemary Lane, Bethnal Green, Shoreditch, and the West of the city. Among them they had 570 pupils attending. Five years later, 40 Ragged Schools were in existence throughout the metropolis, nearly all of which had been started by City Missionaries who continued to devote a considerable amount of time to running them. Initially these schools met only on Sundays, but it was not long before their doors were open on other days of the week.

Crime-worn children

An Edinburgh man, when asked to describe a Ragged School, said they were Sunday schools set up in the poorest parts where every house was *'worn-out and crazy'* and nearly every tenant a beggar, or worse. *'These schools*, he said, *were for ragged, diseased and crime-worn children, such as would not be admitted to any other kind of school.'* The one he instanced was in Field Lane, Smithfield, where 45 young people had to overcome the objections of their parents in order to attend; the parents viewing any possible reformation in their offspring as a potential loss of criminal earnings. Some of the children, who were aged six to 18, had already been in prison, and that, the Scot concluded, would be where they would spend much of the rest of their lives unless educated at the Ragged School. The teacher at Field Lane School was a big-hearted woman who did the work voluntarily three days a week (*Chambers' Edinburgh Journal*, 7th June 1845). According to Shaftesbury, the children who attended Ragged Schools did have at least one advantage over their wealthier contemporaries. *'The thief,'* he said, *'is no fool but is shrewd to a proverb. If we descend to the lowest class of all,* such as the inmates of Ragged Schools, the precocity of these individuals has often been remarked on as little short of a natural phenomenon. Their wits are, in fact, sharpened by their condition, and they are quicker in learning than other individuals, and more easy, in these respects, to be taught.' That may or may not have been the case, but the schools did have some successes.

H.C.T., the son of drunken parents, was one such success. When he first started attending the Ragged School, his brother was already in prison for stealing rather than starving. He was then transported. H.C.T. attended school regularly, behaved well and studied hard. For this he was rewarded with a new pair of shoes and socks, the first he had ever possessed. The following day, in several inches of snow, he appeared at school bare-footed and with his shoes under his arm. So painful were his chilblain-covered feet that he could not wear his new shoes. But he was not prepared to leave them at home for fear his mother would sell them to buy drink. Despite being severely undernourished, H.C.T. was determined not to do as his brother had done, but to make an honest way in life. One day he asked the missionary for the loan of threepence, saying that he could use it to make a living and attend school too. With the threepence he bought a dozen boxes of matches which he sold for sixpence. For nearly two years he attended school all day, sold a dozen boxes of matches in the evening, and lived on his threepence profit. 'When I can read and write well,' he told the missionary, 'I will get a situation.'

While H.C.T. benefited from his years at the Ragged School, there is no suggestion that it made any impact on his home. That was not always the case. One missionary told of two children, a boy and his sister, who were pupils at one of the early Ragged Schools. The pair were so filthy on their first day at school that they needed to be scrubbed and provided with clean clothes, and when they returned home that day their parents hardly recognised them. Their mother was soon to discover that while ragged clothes were no bar to schooling, filth was, and the teachers were strict on the subject of cleanliness. The change in her children began to have some effect on their mother, who started to wash not only their clothes but hers too. Even her husband's shirt found its way into the washtub where it encountered soap for the first time. Her home then began to change till, three months after the children started attending school, it looked a different place. Probably encouraged by the improvement in their home, the boy and girl worked well at school. They took their learning, as well as their cleanliness, home with them, even teaching their parents hymns and verses from the Bible. Their father eventually put away a penny a week to buy his son and daughter a Bible. The change in the family was so marked that even their landlord noticed. So impressed was he, that he offered the father a job as caretaker for all the buildings in the courtyard. Thus the dissipated family was changed through the influence of the Ragged School, and the wretched tenant became the overseer.

Pounds of Portsmouth

Ragged Schools were not just about education. One of the first was run by John Pounds of Portsmouth who, in the 1820s, realised that, to gain the benefit of teaching, a child had first to be fed and clothed, and that for education to be of practical use it had to include some measure of training for employment. Pounds, a cobbler, blazed the trail and many followed. Dr Guthrie opened schools in Edinburgh, Sheriff Watson did the same in Aberdeen, and the LCM missionaries went some way to meet the needs of the tens of thousands of children living in poverty in the metropolis. As late as 1861 the Select Committee on the Education of Destitute Children recognised that educational provision, such as existed, was failing them. *'There exists in many of our great cities and towns a class of children whom the system of national education supported by Parliament, and administered by the Committee of Privy Council for Education, does not reach, and who are excluded, in consequence either of the faults or the misfortunes of their parents, from any participation in its benefits'* (Kathleen Heasman, *Evangelicals in Action*).

By 1861, 176 schools were connected to the Ragged School Union, which for the previous 17 years had worked *'to give permanence, regularity and vigour to the existing Ragged Schools and to promote the formation of new ones'*. Shaftesbury was chairman of the Union. Baptist Noel and R.C.L. Bevan, both closely connected with the London City Mission, were on the committee. So it was not only individual missionaries who were concerned to help the least privileged of the city's children, the Mission's leaders were also working to the same end. Mid-19th century evangelicals had a social conscience that led them to hands-on action; they also had a loud voice that got things done in government. While Shaftesbury was lending his name and support to the Ragged School Union, and visiting individual schools in the poorest parts of London, he was at the same time campaigning for there to be a limit to the number of hours children were allowed to work in factories and coalmines.

To think of Ragged Schools as educational establishments in the modern sense would be wrong. Teachers were, in the main, volunteers, and volunteers with perhaps more heart than expertise. *'The uproar with which anyone visiting such a school would be greeted, the unsavoury remarks, the lewd jokes and general atmosphere of low living would make the visitor immediately aware* (that) *its primary purpose was to reclaim and civilise the child and make him or her a useful member of the community.'*

The LCM's official policy had always been that the spreading of the gospel was paramount, and missionaries were forbidden to be involved financially with their people. As more and more missionaries became involved in the setting up and running of Ragged Schools, the Mission clarified this policy further. '*The missionaries are most carefully to avoid the giving of temporal relief, as not their department of Christian effort, and as most materially interfering with the integrity of their especial work. The missionaries are strictly forbidden from writing letters soliciting aid for persons in distress, or for objects connected with the district, except with the special leave of one of the Secretaries ... The missionaries must not make themselves responsible, or incur pecuniary responsibility in any form, for ... expenses attendant of Ragged Schools, rooms of meeting ...'* Behind these regulations lay not a lack of concern for the poor but the fear that, once missionaries were seen as a source of ready cash, it would be difficult for them to be sure of the honesty of those professing spiritual concern and conversion. The Mission was concerned to avoid the problem of what later became known as 'rice Christians'. Yet the regulations were always interpreted fairly broadly, as in the case of a missionary who persuaded his local butcher and cookshops to help him feed starving children.

It was a feature of the times that men of goodwill spread their favours through many different groups and societies. Lord Shaftesbury supported the London City Mission, the Ragged School Union and over a hundred other societies. In 1867, he and two other peers, Lords Kinnaird (a member of the LCM Committee) and MountTemple, set up the Destitute Children's Dinner Society in response to the desperate need to feed the Ragged School children. Ministers, missionaries, teachers and others of like standing gave needy children a ticket entitling them to a subsidised meal of meat stew, rice and vegetables in one of the many special dining rooms that were opened, several of them attached to Ragged Schools. Funds were set up to help provide for the children in all kinds of ways, not least to give them a party with roast beef and plum pudding each Christmas!

In 1848, Shaftesbury told the Thirteenth Anniversary meeting of the London City Mission, '*It is needless here to discuss what was the origin of Ragged Schools ... We cannot tell where they were born; by God's blessing they exist — by that blessing they will still go forward; but whenever you enter a Ragged School, remember this — we are indebted for nine-tenths of them to the humble, the pious, the earnest City Missionary.*'

Keeping hold of the vision

The London City Mission was not founded to establish Ragged Schools; it had as its great aim to spread the gospel of Jesus Christ throughout the city of London. Even those missionaries whose Journals show their investment of time and interest in the poorest children of their area still had their district to look after. The Committee expected that 36 hours each week would be spent in door-to-door visitation, that time not being inclusive of preparation for and holding meetings, writing Journals and Reports, meeting with local superintendents or any other activity, however commendable. Even Sunday was accounted for. As well as attending two services, missionaries were expected to devote three hours to door-to-door visitation. And the reason the Committee gave for this was that Sunday was the only day of the week on which many men were to be found at home. Apart from that, they felt that the Lord's Day was much the most important day of the week for communicating religious instruction, possibly because some of the people they visited felt it was the day you spoke about God if you spoke about him at all. In short, the work-shy need not apply to the LCM!

The Mission would probably not have been for the nervous or fearful either, as illustrated by one missionary's experience of a visit to a Ragged School. The 'little incident' was reported in the February 1863 Magazine under the heading 'A Missionary Garotted'. *'We fill up the remaining lines of this number with a narrative of a little incident which has just occurred to a missionary ... Having received an invitation to attend a Ragged Shool Meeting in his old district (Deptford), he was induced to accept the invitation and pay a visit to his former friends. His return home from this visit was necessarily somewhat late, and in passing though Southwark near St. Saviour's Church, he was accosted by two men, one of whom pinioned his arms and the other grasped his throat in his embrace. From the effects of the violence he is not yet free. He was robbed by them of his watch and the money which he happened to have in his pockets.'* Interestingly, his watch was returned to him by one of the thieves, but the other had no compunction about keeping a missionary's money!

London City Missionaries have on many occasions been the agents of change, and this was certainly true in the establishment of Ragged Schools. From them, or associated with them, were the Ragged School and Chapel Union (again, with Lord Shaftesbury as its President), the Children's Country Holiday Fund, Pearson's Fresh Air Fund and, more loosely, the National Society for the Prevention of Cruelty to Children.

Thirty years after the first missionaries began Ragged Schools, their work came to an end. With the Education Act of 1870, elementary education was made available for all children, regardless of means. But while children's educational needs were then catered for, their most basic welfare needs were not. The Ragged School Union became the Shaftesbury Society and continued to work for the good of the poorest children. Nor did the London City Mission opt out of education. Missionaries today are still involved in school work, after-school groups and children's clubs. They still have a concern for the whole life of each child.

5

Women in Poverty

'Hell is a city much like London
A populous and smoky city.'
Percy Bysshe Shelley

'In 1865, William Booth was engaged by the East London Special
Services Committee to preach for three weeks in the East End. He
soon founded "The Christian Mission", which, in 1878, became the
Salvation Army.'

'For men must work and women must weep,
And there's little to earn, and many to keep.'
Charles Kingsley

'In the attic of no.10 we found a poor old soul called Granny Evans.
Alone, without fire or food, but with nine "friends" (cats)! What a
terrible sight! We went off to get her warm milk and food. Bought
coal and wood and cleaned up the room. Poor old Granny died a few
days after, of pneumonia and bronchitis.'
LCM Missionary's Journal

'August 30th. I had had a hard day's work, and was returning home
late at night, when just as I had crossed the New Gravel-lane bridge
of the London Docks, I heard a policeman's rattle, and on returning
to the spot was informed that a woman had thrown herself into the
dock. I assisted the constables in getting the drags and searching for
the body. It was more than twenty minutes before it was found. The
divisional surgeon and myself tried for more than an hour to restore

animation, but in vain. *I learned that she was a fallen woman, called "Plymouth Poll", and that she had not been sober for the last three weeks. In all this, I was surrounded by nearly 100 women of a like class with the deceased, who were shrieking, fainting, going into hysterics, then rushing to the public house and pouring gin and rum down their throats, with oaths and blasphemies all around us.'*
LCM Missionary's Journal

Today it is fashionable to speak of 'the feminisation of poverty' – the typical poor person being a divorced or single mother, with limited employment opportunities and poor housing. But in truth, from Ruth and the Widow of Nain in Biblical times to the famine-ridden villages of modern Africa, women have always borne the brunt of poverty. And London in the mid-19th century was certainly no exception. In 1868 a missionary described conditions of his district in the Old Kent Road: *'... the houses are poor, miserable hovels, small, damp, and badly drained; not fit to live in. Some of them have only two rooms. On my first acquaintance with it, the drains did not act, and the yards were filled with filth. When it rained, the slops from the houses, the refuse of the food, rotting vegetables, putrid remains of fish, and the excrements of the people, were swimming about the yards and the streets. Heaps of this kind of rubbish used to lie about the streets, under the burning sun of summer; and to finish the picture, the closets were all open. Women and men might be seen sitting in them as you walked about or sat in the houses ... The people were clothed in rags; and sometimes it could hardly be called clothing. Some of the women had never had a bit of flannel on them since they were born; many of them had no whole garment of any sort.*

In their persons some of these people were as filthy and dirty as their houses. Their skin had lost its colour for want of washing, and their hair was all matted together for want of combing... The odour of the clothes of some of the women when we opened the Mothers' Meeting, and when they got warm in the school, was beyond description ...

Still worse than all this was the state of the children. As for decency, they might as well be naked. ...The children are all more or less diseased. Boils, blains, ulcers and abscesses are to be found in every house of the worst parts of the district ... I have seen boys come to the school door whose old rags of jackets were alive all over them ... (In) Sweep's-alley ... children used to stand at the windows and throw the live things off their persons at strangers as they went about ... In a general way, and taken altogether, the men are cleaner and more respectable than the women ...' The missionary goes on to say that the problem does not seem to be getting any better. *'I am sorry to see that the young women amongst us are as bad as, and, in some cases, worse than the grandmothers.'* He adds that *'drinking and overcrowding are the spring of all the evils peculiar to the worst parts of London'*, and he views the overcrowded housing as being perhaps the root problem. Their *'vices are nurtured by the state in which they live. The overcrowding is awful.'*

A missionary describing his district along the Gray's Inn Road repeated the same message the following year. High rents (fuelled by demolitions of old properties) meant that most families could not afford more than one room, which had to serve all purposes not only for a man, woman and their children, but often also for a married daughter and her family. Infested with vermin, such conditions were literal breeding-grounds for all kinds of disease.

'I'm going out!'

For many, including the women, the only place of escape was the local pub or ginpalace, with its warm taproom, glittering decorations, and reasonably comfortable seats. The bar, and the company of friends and neighbours, was *'an irresistible attraction to allure and detain the poor man and woman from the comfortless, untidy, dirty rooms they call their homes'*. However, the heavy-drinking culture of the pub only worsened the poverty of such families. Working men considered that once they had given 'the wife' a number of shillings as the week's allowance for the home, they were entitled to spend everything else they earned *'at once, without care for future contingencies'*. With her allowance in her hands, and her man drinking at the local ginpalace, the wife would go straight to the pawnbroker's to redeem as much as she could of the clothes and household items that she had pawned during the previous week, trying to tide the family over until pay-day.

'*It is usual,*' writes the same missionary, '*for the husband and children who are at work to place that portion of their earnings allotted to the household expenses in the hands of the missus, and, so long as the customary meals and other necessities are forthcoming at the proper time, the man cares not to be bothered by the details of expenses; he leaves all that, he says, to the missus.*' For many women, managing the household budget was impossible apart from the local pawnshop and the loanshark. Every week, but especially in times of unemployment and other hardships, items of clothing, cutlery, furniture – even the beds and bedclothes – and anything else that would raise cash, were taken along to the pawnshop. All being well, they could be redeemed on the Saturday evening. But when this proved impossible, more desperate measures were tried. Many poor women earned a pittance by taking in laundry each week from nearby well-to-do households. Some then pawned the middle-class linen, planning to redeem it in time to return it when the weekly collection and delivery was made. But if something went wrong, and there was no money for the redemption, a further step on the ladder of debt was frequently taken. The pawnshop loans included a high interest rate, but the 'loan and discount society' charged even more. Advertising in the local bars, it seemed to offer an easy way of escape from the harrowing troubles of poverty. In reality, it only trapped the borrower in worse debt. The missionary supplies an example, showing how someone taking out a loan of £4, repaid in weekly instalments of 2 shillings, would actually end up repaying £5 2s 2d, and would in any case, only receive

£2 17s 10d in cash, because of various costs involved in getting the loan in the first place.

This downward spiral of economic entrapment was extremely difficult to escape from. Indeed, *'people who are in such difficulties try, also, might and main to involve others in the same difficulties as their own. If a young married woman comes to reside in a house she is waylaid and tempted in every possible way by her neighbour'* who will, unless she is quick-witted, *'bring her down to their customs, circumstances and miseries.'* Many wives were lucky if they received even a few shillings on a Saturday night. Some men never got beyond the dock-gate pub before the entire week's wages had been consumed in liquid form. Others seldom saw any wages at all because of unemployment or sickness for which there was not yet the safety net of a Welfare State. And, of course, there were some (only a minority, according to the missionaries) who were too lazy to work – like the Bethnal Green man whose wife told John Galt, *'My old man's an expert on work. He knows exactly where to look for it where he won't find it – and where it won't find him!'*

Faced with such uncertain income, many women tried to eke out their income by legal employment. But the conditions and rewards were sparse. In addition to those who took in laundry, some walked miles to scrub and polish the doorsteps of the wealthy. Others worked at home, stuffing horse-hair mattresses, making matchboxes, or sewing garments. While London (unlike Manchester and other industrial towns) had few large factories, there were many sweatshops. Remuneration, whether at home or in the sweatshop, was usually by piece-rate. In the 1890s, home-based matchbox makers received two-and-a-half pence for 144 matchboxes, with the workers having to pay for glue, twine and brushes, and to fetch the materials for the boxes. Working 16 or 18 hours, most workers earned less than one shilling a day. As late as 1913, women sewing cycling shorts reckoned they could earn one penny an hour – and still had to provide their own thread!

Desperate measures

But not all women could find or cope with such work. Some ended up in the Workhouse, where the communal conditions were deliberately kept as unattractive as possible. These Workhouses were another early target for visitation by City Missionaries, although sometimes they were refused permission because of denominational rivalries among the churches. For many women the only available income was through prostitution. Especially around the docks, where sailors came ashore with months of backpay, women congregated in gin-palaces and cheap theatres and sought to attract business. A nearby missionary reported at least 2,000 such women in his district. But throughout the impoverished areas of the city, desperate people resorted to selling themselves, or even their relatives. The missionary to a district near Tottenham Court Road reported meeting an Irish family where the father and mother sent their daughter out to work as a prostitute in order to survive.

In many cases it was not simple economic desperation that drove women, but the cruelty of 'respectable' society. Many became street women because, while servants in middle- or upper-class houses, they had been seduced by their masters or by fellowservants. Pregnant, they were instantly dismissed, and without a good reference were doomed to abject poverty. Ashamed to return to their own families, such girls very easily fell into the hands of pimps and madams. They could be as young as 14. For many, life on the streets, despite the gaudy glamour, involved brutal violence and constant squalor. Suicide was a frequent last resort, and the bridge in Gravel Lane — renamed 'The Bridge of Sighs' by the local missionary — was permanently manned by a police constable as a deterrent.

From its very beginning the LCM had a real concern for such 'fallen women' and campaigned for the provision of more 'penitentiaries' and 'refuges' for them. Though their regime might seem Spartan to us, such institutions offered the only realistic alternative to life on the streets. Estimates varied as to the numbers of prostitutes in London, but all agreed that there were many thousands of women involved. One missionary reported that, in his small district alone, *'there are nearly 350 furnished rooms occupied for the most part by strange women'*.

For all their Christian abhorrence of sin, the missionaries who worked in poor districts of the city displayed a great deal of sympathy and understanding for such women. The 1849 Annual Report tells the story of a girl who went on the streets at the age of 13, and twice relapsed after being taken back home by her widowed mother. But a missionary who met and befriended her, and then was able to reconcile mother and daughter, found the girl a place in a refuge and eventually helped her to become a church member and to get a job. In one year, Missionary Thomas Jackson reported that '*227 fallen females had visited him at his own house, imploring him to aid them in reforming their character and commencing a virtuous course of life*'. From 1859 'Midnight Meetings' were held, providing tea and a Christian message (Baptist Noel was the speaker at the very first of these), together with the offer of immediate admission to a Refuge. Encouraged by the LCM, many organisations were founded to rescue such women and to provide accommodation and training for them, and although John

Weylland wrote that '*in no department of Christian effort are there more frequent and cruel disappointments,*' he could add, '*the known results are more than encouraging. The records of the work give proof of hundreds of the saved (from the streets) being now happy Christian women, some of whom are exceptionally earnest in Christian work.*'

The London City Mission's ministry to the wider population of women in the impoverished districts of London took many forms, often relying on women workers. For although the society had decided (for purely practical reasons) to recruit only male missionaries, the Mission always recognised and relied on the active involvement of women as volunteer helpers and visitors. When Mrs Ranyard founded her society of Biblewomen to visit, help and read the Bible to the poor, the City Missionaries worked in close co-operation with them. A prominent feature was the Mothers' Meeting, with training in sewing and household skills, and also a maternity basket with essential clothes and supplies to be loaned to new mothers. A young, single missionary was highly embarrassed, when going to a new district in Poplar in the 1890s, to discover that there was no-one but him to lead the Mothers' Meeting and inspect new-born babies. He recognised the only remedy – and soon found a wife! Such meetings obviously touched a real need – the Mothers' Meeting on the Old Kent Road attracted about 200 women and girls during the course of 1868, and the results were evident. '*There has been a great improvement in the outward appearance of the people, and of the babies the women bring with them; and this is not because they are a better-off class of people, but because the same class are more clean and decent than when they first came. They try to have shoes, gowns and bonnets, and to have their hands and faces washed and their hair combed. Some of them, however, still have no beds and no furniture in the room.*'

In addition, the LCM used and encouraged a wide range of practical and spiritual helps to deal with both the immediate and the underlying problems of women in poverty. In the Kensington Potteries area of West London, missionary Michael Parfitt served from 1851 until 1878, assisted by a Mrs Bayly, author of 'Ragged Homes and How to Mend Them' and no doubt a formidably able Victorian woman. Among the products of that ministry were: a Ragged School for girls; provision of drains, running water and gas to the district; soup kitchens; a system for loaning whitewash brushes for the poor to paint their rooms; a 'Public House without the Drink'; night school for adults; musical entertainment evenings; excursions to the countryside; and several Mission Halls and churches.

Not all women who found themselves in need came from an impoverished background, as John Farley recounts in his *Tales of the City*. *'A woman came, bowed with grief, and told the following story, "My father was a minister of the Gospel; he and my mother died. I obtained a situation as amanuensis in the family of Lady —, and remained there until her ladyship's decease. She bequeathed me £1,000. With the money I purchased a business in the Berlin wood and fancy trade in Oxford Street ... A commercial traveller who called for orders sought my acquaintance, and shortly after he made me an offer of marriage, which I accepted — alas! afterwards to rue; for I discovered he was a drunkard. Three months after our marriage he one day disappeared. A week later, two men came into the shop, and produced a document which proved that my husband had sold the business, stock, and furniture; so that I was deserted, destitute, and homeless ... I took lodgings at Hoxton, and last Sunday week, after brooding over my calamity, I gave way to despair and resolved to end all by throwing myself into the canal. On my way to accomplish the deed I passed your hall; the hymn you were singing arrested my attention. It was my father's favourite hymn and tune."'* The same thing prevented her ending her life the following week, and in the months that followed the woman found peace, just a short time before she died in childbirth.

City Missionaries did not share the attitude of many Victorians that women were essentially angelic, with almost all the problems of society being caused by drunken and immoral men. Their reports described drunkenness among women, and cases of husband-beating as well as wife-beating. Missionaries did not by any means limit their ministry to women and children, as some Christians have tended to do. But alongside their attempts to reach, educate, and save the men of London, they constantly and realistically addressed the problems and needs of the city's women. Running through all their concern and efforts to provide practical help was the firm and central conviction that a personal conversion to faith in Jesus Christ was the single most important need, whatever their situation and problems. Concluding his report in 1869, the missionary to the Gray's Inn Road district says: '*I could fill several pages were I to give a detailed account of the ways in which the (poor) have attempted to cling to me for help. What secular remedies are requisite it is not for me to inquire. But I am quite certain that not any measure can prove successful which is unaccompanied with the co-operation of the poor themselves. The remedy is the Gospel, for where that is received truly into the heart it carries conversion, both in temporal and spiritual things ... Whenever men or women, young or old, believe in the Lord Jesus Christ, their lives will present the practical effects. And conversion in every instance produces a change of character and a corresponding change in outward appearance, and very soon places the people in different circumstances. They become provident and cleanly.*'

The missionaries were well enough in touch with reality to know that such conversions did not usually come easily.

Summing up his Old Kent Road district a year earlier, the missionary wrote: '*Whatever success I may have had in the school or the meetings, I owe it to the household visitation. The general visitation brings the children to the school — it brings the mothers to the Meeting, and the fathers and the mothers to the temperance entertainment. But more than all, it is this which gives me the attendance at the religious meetings. Without the house to house visitation I could do no good among the people.*' Yet, despite a few hopeful cases, he adds, '*What there is most to contend with here is not the opposition of bad principles, but of a bad life. Low habits are the things which separate men from God amongst us. The entire forgetfulness of a better world, except for a few minutes when somebody dies. Plenty to eat and drink, with every means of indulgence to the flesh. This is the highest idea they entertain of Paradise — either in this world or the next.*'

6

Workplace Missionaries

'I love the London City Mission because it takes the glorious Gospel direct to the people. Thank God for all faithful preaching in churches and chapels, but the multitudes are outside. Oh! support this Mission because it takes Jesus and His salvation to the perishing. It is a grand personal ministry. God bless and prosper it, more and more.'
C. H. Spurgeon

'There are two things for which I especially love the LCM. Firstly, its loyalty to the old Gospel of our Lord Jesus Christ. Secondly, because of its house to house, yea, person to person work. I believe more and more in soul to soul work. Personal dealing is the main thing and I believe God will increasingly own and bless this special work of the Mission and bring thousands to the feet of Jesus, who will be gathered into the churches of this great city.'
The Rt Hon. Lord Kinnaird

Summaries of the Work of the London City Mission, and its results, during the year 1874-5

Number of missionaries	437
Visits paid	2,607,809
Of which to the sick and dying	275,795
Scriptures distributed	7,688
Religious tracts distributed	3,512,775
Books lent	53,405

Indoor meetings and Bible classes held	*38,647*
Average attendance at ditto	*49*
Gross attendance at ditto	*1,926,764*
Additional indoor meetings in factories,	
workhouses, penitentiaries, etc.	*17,588*
Gross attendance at ditto	*562,052*
Persons visited or conversed with	
in factories, etc	*206,581*
Outdoor services held	*5,163*
Average attendance at ditto	*61*
Gross attendance at ditto	*316,181*
New communicants	*1,689*
Restored to Church Communion	*293*
Drunkards reclaimed	*1,625*
Unmarried couples induced to marry	*274*
Fallen women admitted to asylums, restored	
to their homes, or otherwise rescued	*617*

LCM Annual Report, 1875

*Following the International Exhibitions in Paris, in 1867 and 1878,
to which the LCM had sent missionaries, on 23rd June, 1879, a
Paris City Mission, modelled on the LCM, was founded at a meeting
at 23, Rue Royale.*

The London City Mission's policy of appointing missionaries to geographical areas that they visited in a systematic way could have limited its usefulness mainly to the women of the capital as they were at home with children or working from home. But from just eight years after its foundation in 1835, the LCM placed missionaries where the working men were. London's economy has been based on trading from its very beginning, with the Thames as the main artery carrying its life-blood. Goods arriving by ship at the various London docks went further afield on carts, canal boats, and (later) trains. And the traffic was two-way, with manufactured goods being carried from as far north as the Midlands to the Thames for shipment.

As the city expanded, the newly rich moved further from its centre, commuting into town each day. Necessity bred invention and, in 1829, omnibuses – three-horse vehicles carrying 20 passengers – went into service, to be followed in 1836 by the railway. Thirty-four years later the first horse-drawn tram companies received authorisation, one of them carrying a million passengers in its first six months. The traffic problems today are not very different to those of the mid 19th century. The need for quicker and more efficient transport brought jobs. Men were needed to lay roads and railtracks, to build bridges and tunnels. They got jobs as cabbies and omnibus drivers, railwaymen and canal boatmen. And the ever-expanding docks absorbed a workforce of hundreds of thousands.

Going where the men are

The London City Mission, looking at the changes happening all around and seeing a mission-field, by the 1870s had placed men in a long list of workplaces. Among others, they served bakers, cabmen and coachmen, drovers and omnibusmen, factory workers, letter carriers and night cabmen, the police and soldiers. The docks were central to the very existence of London, and the LCM went into the docks to reach sailors and dockers with its message. Entering a typical dock from East Smithfield, one missionary picked his way among hundreds of barrels of sherry on his right and 'stupendous' warehouses of wool, tea, spice and drugs on his left. At the North Quay he would find one day splendid clippers, 'models of beauty', which had brought in wool, tallow, hides, preserved meats, copper etc., and another day ships carrying 30,000 to 40,000 chests of tea. Then there were the Spanish steamers with cargoes of oranges, lead and cork; and ships from further afield laden with dried fruits, cocoa nibs, tobacco and much else besides. The South Quay often had English steamers with their French brandy, generally a thousand ton cargo at a time. At the West Quay he might find up to 20 outward-bound vessels loading. Sailors were there from Europe, the Far and Near East, Scandinavia, the Americas and even Australia. And that was just one of London's many docks.

One can almost feel the excitement of the man, as this missionary wrote his report. *'Not only Spain and Portugal, but the colonies of Cuba and the Philippine Isles, as also the kingdoms and republics of South America, which once owned the sway of these mother countries, send their representatives here. The short stunted Manilla, the black woolly-headed Columbian, the half Indian Chileno, Brazilian, Mexicans, and others, all understanding the Spanish language thrust upon them by their conquerors, and all having received from them their religion also, are, through the means of that same language, brought under the sound of the Gospel by the agency of the London City Mission.'* And English sailors were not forgotten, the LCM held the gospel out to them with equal enthusiasm.

Missionaries were required to keep a detailed statistical account of their work. However much of a drudge at the time, the resulting figures make for interesting reading over a hundred years later. One missionary working in the docks was able to board 824 English vessels in a year, and to speak to 3,500 English seamen. But he had to be careful not to overstep the mark. *'As there are always numbers of men on board who are loading, repairing, or doing other work, a word may be spoken with them, but as much fear exists lest the men should cease work, great caution needs to be exercised when to speak and when to be silent.'* Missionaries had to be cautious about interrupting the men's labours, for most of the dockers were day labourers, and if they were found slacking they would not be employed again. There were always plenty outside the dock gates each morning waiting to take their place. Even there, as the missionary came and went from his day's work, he did not miss his opportunities. In addition to the would-be workers there were about a hundred gatemen and constables to whom he could speak.

George Gillman worked for 50 years as an LCM missionary to foreign sailors, and his unpublished reminiscences let us walk with him through the docks and along Ratcliff Highway, a notorious area frequented by sailors. *'Here the Gin Palaces, Restaurants and Cafés are gaily dressed and filled with foreign and English seamen in all costumes, here are Italian and Austrian seamen in groups 20 or 30 in number promenading accompanied by women dressed in gay colours. Yonder is a string of Chinamen in native dress. Pigtail, paper boots, petticoats and umbrella included. One behind the other following like a flock of sheep the leader who is taking them to the opium room or gambling house. Close by are a group of Spaniards, of Portuguese, South Americans and Manilamen just come ashore and already they are in the hands of the dragons of the street, who with a shuttle cock, ball or skipping rope will make their stay on shore apparently pleasant. But leaving as is usual the sting behind, money gone, or ... worse.'*

Seamen going on shore were good news to the local opportunists, for the men would have money in their pockets. They were enticed into shops full of gaudy handkerchiefs, brightly coloured umbrellas, 'gold' watches and other suitable gifts for taking home, and in these they spent some of their money. What was left was often divided between drink and women who would relieve them of the goods they had bought, resell them to the shops where they would be purchased by the sailors from the next ship to dock. This recycling was the trade of Ratcliff Highway. Gillman walked the Highway speaking to sailors and inviting them to services that were held in Spanish, the lingua franca of most of the seamen. But he did not stop at that in his efforts to reach them with the Gospel, nor did he confine himself to Spanish. In one morning's work, he boarded an Austrian vessel with a crew of Slavonians to whom he read a portion of the New Testament in Italian. From there he went to the *Vercingetorix*, a French ship, then to the *Oporto* with its Portuguese crew. From the *Oporto* he headed for the Spanish *Lista* on which he held a short service before going ashore and visiting on the Highway. In the course of his long service to foreign seamen, Gillman gave out thousands of New Testaments to men from countries in which a vernacular Bible was then unknown or forbidden, and he had the joy of knowing that some had come to faith through reading them.

On the factory floor

Many of the ships that George Gillman saw leaving the docks lay low in the water, heavy with goods manufactured in England. And the factory workers had their missionaries too. In the early 1870s, the Camden Town missionary was appointed to the visitation of the factories of that entire parish, some of which were small back-street affairs while others were larger and more organised. Employers who, doubtless, sometimes saw his visits as a time-wasting exercise did not always meet him with enthusiasm. But in his Journal we read that he gained access to 180 factories with about 2,400 men and boys employed in them. Camden Town seems to have been a centre for the production of musical instruments as he lists organ builders, pianoforte and harmonium makers among those he visited, along with engineers, smiths, cabinetmakers, gas-meter makers, braziers and zinc workers.

There were agitators then as there are now, and the missionary came up against them. The Camden Town missionary wrote of a lunch-time visit he paid to one factory, where he met 20 to 30 men, the majority of whom were *'professed infidels, followers of Bradlaugh, and readers of "The National Reformer"'*. They met him with objection after objection, mingled with awful blasphemy, and gave him no chance whatever of replying to their objections. On his second visit the factory time-keeper greeted him with the comment that he hoped the missionary would do some good in the factory as the agitators were 'poison' to the rest of the workers. By his third visit, he was allowed to read a short passage of Scripture, and soon he was heartily welcome and able to *'hold quiet Scripture readings with different groups of men, and have fair arguments with the sceptics'*. The missionary to the Midland Railway Stables met with a different reception as there were some Christian men among the workforce. He was able to reinforce their witness and, with their support, held a short service in the lunch break.

Another missionary, who visited factories in the Bromley-by-Bow district, wrote a vivid description of the circumstances in which many people worked. *'Here I found about 1,000 visitable families of the poorest description, the great majority of them earning a crust in the numerous factories around. Some of them were engaged in making matches in the match factory; some in preparing patent manure of the blood which various butchers' shops in London supplied, and of the decaying fish of Billingsgate, and other markets; some were employed in making Harper Twelvetrees' soap-powder, which was advertised as capable of "making homes happy, curing bad tempers, keeping children from crying, making washing-day a pleasure."Etc. Others were employed in the rag factory, in various chemical factories, in manufacturing gas, prussic acid, tar, naphtha, India-rubber, starch, coke, Etc.; and others found something to do in the market-gardens, the docks, the distilleries and malt-house. From these numerous scenes of labour,'* he concludes – and we can almost see his face as he writes – *'it will be readily perceived that a combination of smells was produced very disagreeable to the olfactory organ, and not at all calculated to add much oxygen to the atmosphere.'*

In the Golden Lane district of the capital, a missionary visited what seems an even more diverse set of factories. He held a regular service for 200 women in a ladies' clothing firm, another for 100 women and 20 men in a factory making fancy boxes. Fifty men and 40 women making envelopes were visited regularly as were the workers in his local artificial flower manufactory. Some owners, who were Christians, welcomed him, even providing Moody and Sankey hymn books so that their workers could join in singing. When this missionary wrote an article for the LCM magazine, he noted that he had not seen many cases of conversion through his factory visits, but believed that seed had been sown in many hearts and that, by God's grace, it could take root. Although missionaries rejoiced when they saw the fruits of their labours, theirs was no quick-fix job. There were sudden conversions without doubt, but most of their work was in the nature of a faithful slog.

While these two men were working in Bromley-by-Bow and Camden Town, another resident of London was coming to the end of his burst of activity among the workers of the city. Karl Marx, who arrived in England in 1849, had added his voice to the discontent and the missionaries often met his followers as they went on their rounds. Unrest that had sparked into violence in the second half of the 1860s, between followers of the young trade union movement and those who opposed it, resulted in the Royal Commission on Trade Unions in 1867. That same year the Reform Act gave more workers the right to vote, extending the franchise to lodgers in rooms worth at least £10, who had lived at one address for a year. Despite the Commission reporting positively about trade unionism, and the electorate of London rising from 180,000 to 304,000 because of the Reform Act, it was to be another eight years before peaceful picketing became legal and the threat of criminal prosecution for breach of contract was removed from strikers. Although Marx's thinking rumbled away like distant thunder, it did not break into a memorable storm, possibly in part because London had few big factories. Despite the hundreds of thousands of working men in London, by the early 1880s union membership was tiny: the compositors' and engineers' unions each had around 6,000 members in the metropolis; the tailors, bricklayers and carpenters about 2,000 each; and railway workers, bootmakers, boiler-makers and stonemasons only in the region of 1000. The next 40 years were to change that dramatically.

Reaching out to railwaymen

Meanwhile, the London City Mission's men continued their visitation of workplaces. One of the mushrooming industries from the 1840s onwards was that of the railways. It is hard to take in what the coming of the railway did to England in terms of ease of travel and transport of manufactured products, but even harder to conceive of its impact on the capital. Between 1835 and 1870 a dozen or more major railways dug and built their ways into central London. In the process, large areas of mostly slum property were demolished. The more affluent used the railway to allow them to live in the greener suburbs of the city. A great movement began that led, eventually, to the depopulation of the city centre.

Because the LCM has always placed its men where people are, the Mission was not slow to put men into the railway industry. Some were even supported by railway companies. The London and North-Western Railway funded its own missionary, based at the Euston terminus. The work he did among the thousand or so porters, guards, signallers, shunters, cleaners, sweepers, messengers, carpenters, painters, trimmers, washers, platelayers, blacksmiths, whitesmiths, lamp cleaners, fitters, lifters, writers, omnibus and parcel-cart and van drivers and conductors, cabmen, engine drivers, firemen and polishers (and their families) was typical of other missionaries in the industry. His was an evangelistic job and a pastoral one too. While he spoke to men about their souls, and preached when the opportunity arose, he also drew alongside them in times of trouble. In heavy industry, before health and safety standards were an issue, there was trouble aplenty at work, and in the days before antibiotics and the National Health Service there was often heartbreak at home too.

It would do the London City Mission a great disservice to picture its workers as cold, unfeeling men who preached hell-fire at whoever was within earshot. That was far from the case. Most missionaries were from working-class backgrounds, some even with experience in the industries they ministered to. They knew very well that they had to earn the right to speak by gaining the respect of the ordinary workers. Workplace missionaries were not managers' men, they had hearts for the lowliest and the highest in the trade, believing that rich and poor alike needed to hear the gospel and come to Jesus Christ.

The London and North-Western Railway gained from its missionary, as did those who worked for it, when he was cast in the role of peacemaker in a dispute in 1872–3, though he played down the effect of his personal contribution. On the matter of strikes, he says, '*Here a Christian visitor has an opportunity for stepping in as the peacemaker, and if he be known to and respected by the strikers, his influence can hardly be over-estimated … In some departments the men have had their wages raised, apparently without an angry word on either side, and now the porters have come to feel their need of an increase in their pay, owing to the high price of food, fuel, and other necessaries, but there has been no clamorous demand for what they may think is their rights. They have petitioned the Board of Directors in very respectful terms to raise their wages for the above reasons, and it is gratifying to know that whether I have had anything to do with the respectful and orderly way in which this thing has been done or not, they have acted upon my advice.*'

Much of a railway missionary's work was visitation, similar in many ways to the door-to-door work of his district colleagues. The man based at King's Cross in 1876, noted that the guards' room, situated under the booking office at King's Cross; the washers' room, near York Road Station; the porters' room, above one of the goods banks; the coffee rooms – one for the clerks employed, one for the foremen, and one for the porters, all near the goods bank; the infirmary room at the end of the railway yard, and attended by those who look after the sick horses belonging to the company; and the locomotive mess-room, as well as the engineers' shops, were all among his regular ports of call. And that work is still being carried on in more of less the same way today – minus the horses!

The London City Mission has an unbroken record of service to railway workers from the 1840s to the present day. Inevitably missionaries have been called to help at times of tragedy, both personal and when there have been rail disasters. When an engine driver slipped and fell beneath the train's wheels in 1887, he died at the scene. Another driver, going to his aid, had his arm torn off and also died. There were no professional counsellors in those days, but the LCM was there and available to colleagues and families. Sixty six years later, when England suffered one of its worst rail accidents, with 112 people killed and 183 severely injured at Harrow, missionaries were there again. *'I know that this was no time for preaching,'* Arthur Oldham, missionary to British Railways, said, *'but as I listened to stories of marvellous escapes, met anxious people, I was able to pass on the appropriate word. When my work at the station was over, I had the sad task of visiting the hospitals, the bereaved and attending several funerals each day.'*

And lest we forget that the men who work for others have problems of their own, think of this 19th century railway missionary's heavy heart as he set out to work each day. *'A thick cloud darkened my home, and deep sorrow filled my heart as the object of my youthful affection, the partner of my life, lay in the cold embrace of death, leaving myself and five children to mourn her loss … The scenes of suffering and calamity amongst which I have had to mingle occasionally ... broken limbs and broken hearts ... I have felt their influence keenly.'*

Although docks, factories and railways are but three of the industries to which the London City Mission has devoted its manpower, in many ways they are typical and give a flavour of the whole. The lists of workplace missionaries, given in each Annual Report, provide an indicator of the city's economy and of the LCM's growth. The 1910 list is as follows:

Bakers, day and night cabmen, firemen, dockers, drovers, gasmen, letter-carriers, sailors, soldiers, railwaymen, navvies, policemen, brickfield workers, workers in public houses and coffee-shops, omnibusmen, canal boatmen, club-house servants, coachmen, motor drivers, stablemen and grooms, coalies and carmen, slaughtermen, factory workers, theatre and music-hall employees, hotel and restaurant servants, millers, public works employees, tramcarmen, postal and telegraph employees, dining-room workers, scavengers, workers at Billingsgate and Smithfield Markets.

7

Housing and Homelessness

'If the achievements of the LCM have not made London a city of saints, yet, by the blessing of God, they have undoubtedly saved it from becoming a city of devils. I know of no Mission doing such a widespread and efficacious work.'
Lord Shaftesbury

'We do not say the condition of their homes, for how can those places be called homes, compared with which the lair of a wild beast would be a comfortable and healthy spot? Few who will read these pages have any conception of what these pestilential human rookeries are, where tens of thousands are crowded together amidst horrors which call to mind what we have heard of the middle passage of the slave ship...'
Andrew Mearns, 'The Bitter Cry of Outcast London', 1883

'"There have been at work among us", a Nonconformist preacher told his people, 'three great social agencies: the London City Mission; the novels of Mr. Dickens; the cholera."'
G.M. Young, *Portrait of an Age*, 1936

'A "good" meal for a man, wife and five children — Trotters, 2d; cow-heel pieces, 1d, potherbs, 1d, potatoes, 1½d; in all, 5½ d. ... Two sisters, both widows, one blind, clean and steady, live on 2½d a day each.'
The LCM Magazine, Aug. 1887

My '*district is now undergoing some changes, in consequence
of the demolition of old houses for the formation of new streets
in one part, and for the erection of a Board school in another.*'
City Missionary, 1883

In many ways the 1880s was a decade of change in London, but not all of it was for the better. Every new road and railway involved the demolition of more slums. Because there was no obligation to house those made homeless, they drifted into already overcrowded areas and compounded the problems there. The metropolis housed its richest and poorest just a stone's throw from each other. Behind the fine homes of the privileged, with their varnished doors and gleaming lace-curtained windows, were the alleys where slum dwellers lived in unspeakable conditions, and where the newly homeless pushed in and looked for a place to settle.

The rookeries of London

Some of the houses — known as rookeries — that were demolished in the name of progress were notorious. The Rev. Thomas Beames' book *The Rookeries of London* had been quoted in the LCM Magazine in 1852. '*Doubtless there is some analogy between these pauper colonies and the nests of the birds from which they take their name; the houses for the most part high and narrow, the largest possible number crowded into a given space ... In one house 100 persons have been known to sleep on a given night. In a particular instance, we ascertained that three rooms were thus occupied — first room, by eight persons; second, by fifteen; third, by twenty-four ... In these rooms are piled the wares by which some of the inhabitants gain their precarious living, — oranges, herrings, water-cresses, onions, seemed to be the most marketable articles ...*' Shaftesbury told of a visit he made to such a slum. Having been informed that five families lived together in one room, a family in each corner and one in the middle, he asked how they managed it. '*Oh*,' was the reply, '*we did very well until the family in the middle took in a lodger.*'

Rookeries and other tenement slums often had their own security systems to prevent unwelcome callers such as the landlord and the police. Their stairways were narrow, dark and often without handrails. Occasional steps had their supports removed so that the unsuspecting fell through them as they climbed. Residents knew exactly which steps to avoid. More than one missionary came a cropper in an effort to visit the homes in his district. But it was not only the very poor who could be less than friendly to the men from the Mission – as one of them, John Hunt, remembered. *'I was insulted, laughed at and treated with the coldest indifference. When I knocked at a door, up went an upstair window, and a head could be seen, demanding with some rudeness, "What do you want?" At other times the front door opened just ajar, and no sooner was my errand made known, than the door was slammed in my face, and again I was compelled to go further on. How to get at the people, especially the more respectable, in their own homes, was to me no easy matter to discover. All kinds of dodging and scheming, even to sarcasm and guile, were resorted to, to prevent me from presenting a personal and pointed Gospel.'* The homes Hunt visited would be thought crowded by today's standards, but they were nothing compared to the inhuman conditions in the rookeries.

The Rev. Andrew Mearns, Secretary of the London Congregational Union, was the main author of 'The Bitter Cry of Outcast London'. In it he said, *'One of the saddest results of this overcrowding is the inevitable association of honest people with criminals. Often is the family of an honest working man compelled to take refuge in a thieves' kitchen ... Who can wonder that evil flourishes in such hotbeds of vice and disease? ... Incest is common; and no form of vice or sensuality causes surprise or attracts attention ... The low parts of London are the sink into which the filthy and abominable from all parts of the country seem to flow.'* This twenty-page pamphlet, which was first published in 1883, caused an outcry. But it was not a lone voice. A series of articles were, at the same time, being published in the *Pictorial World* on the subject 'How the poor live'. In them, George Sims introduced his readers to '*a dark continent that is within easy walking distance of the General Post Office* (close to St. Paul's Cathedral).'

Thieves welcome

John Hunt obviously persisted despite the rebuffs, and it seems that his stand was eventually respected, if in an unlikely quarter. '*I had a meeting specially for thieves. This was more strictly guarded than any of the other meetings; none but known thieves being admitted. They made me their confidant, and found in the City Missionary what they called "A true friend". I helped them over many a formidable difficulty, when seeking a reformation of life. Some overwise friends called me a "crack-brained fanatic". But what of that, if only I could lay the spoils of victory — souls won — at the feet of Him on whose head are many crowns? The penitent thief, who died at the Saviour's side, is by no means the only thief ransomed by Divine grace. A good number of the thieves and criminals were saved in the slums of the Mint* (his area). *The meeting room was more frequently crowded to excess than otherwise, and what I considered a remarkable fact was this — by request of these wretchedly poor people I nailed up a money-box in the room in which they could put a farthing, or a halfpenny, as the case might be, and received in one year 19s 7¾d, mostly in farthings, and no thief ever attempted to touch it.*'

Another reason for increased overcrowding was described by the Missionary in the Hague Street district of Bethnal Green when he presented his Annual Report in 1887. He told of already full houses that had become even more overcrowded when slums were pulled down to allow for the building of homes for wealthier people. Within the space of a year the population of his district increased dramatically. Urban regeneration is a cyclical thing, and LCM is now old enough to have seen several complete cycles. Having worked at the end of the 19th century with those living in appalling housing conditions, missionaries had the joy of seeing new homes being built and occupied. Many of these have become the slums of today, their tenants are the poor of today, and their needs and challenges are the same as they were all those years ago.

Homeless – then and now

Homelessness in our cities is a big issue at the beginning of the 21st century, and both the state and charities do what they can to meet the needs of those who live on the streets. But it is no new problem. John Weylland, in LCM's April 1890 Magazine, described a scene that sounds remarkably contemporary. According to him, among the facts of life in London at that time was that tens of thousands of men and women were homeless. Common-lodging houses were merely shelters for those who could occasionally gather together a few pence for a little comfort before being out on the streets again the next morning. These homeless people came from all parts of the country, as well as from the continent and even further afield. Many of them, he stated, were from what he called the criminal class, but among them he found people from respectable families who had been '*beaten down in the struggle of life*'.

Police statement

Nearly 40 years previously the Police Commissioner acknowledged the work done by the LCM in lodging houses. '*In visiting houses of this character it is impossible but to consider whether some moral or religious influence cannot be applied to benefit the outcasts of society; but this work* has been begun by the City Mission, and it will be to the honour of the Society, and all who support it, to continue its labours amongst those who stand so much in need of it, and whose condition has hitherto been so sadly neglected.' The Police Commissioner was not the only one to see what the missionaries where doing, and where they were doing it. Lord Shaftesbury visited lodging houses with Messrs Miller, Walker and Jackson, three men from the Mission. He was so stirred by what he saw, heard and smelt, that he pulled out all the stops and forced new legislation through Parliament that placed lodging houses under the inspection of the police. The Act limited the number of residents according to the size of the building, separated the sexes, and made provision for the restraint of criminals. As a consequence of the Act, common-lodging houses greatly increased in number but the conditions within them began to improve. In 1890, it was estimated that 50,000 people were in the city's lodging houses each night, with more than a quarter of them being under 15 years of age.

In 1884, the LCM's Magazine carried a report of a visit to the Asylum for the Houseless Poor in Banner Street, St. Luke's. *'Gaining the entrance hall, I watch their admission. I notice that some present have white tickets and others green. The former, I am told, indicate those who come for the first time; if they are accepted, their ticket gives them the privilege of remaining here for seven nights. After this they cannot be admitted again for fourteen days. ... Their names entered, they pass on into the dormitories, receiving, as they go, each one the eighth part of a quartern loaf of wholesome bread ... I confess that this seemed to me at first a very cold and cheerless kind of charity, and I am not sure that I am yet reconciled to the notion of such strictly limited philanthropy. The purpose of the regulation is admirable enough; it is to make sure that no inducement shall be offered to laziness and unworthiness, and, also, that the relief, such as it is, may be given to as large a number as possible of the really homeless poor ... There are five (wards) — two for men, two for women, and one for children, or women having little children in their care. These wards, which are scrupulously clean, lighted with gas, and warmed by hot-water pipes, contain 50 to 200 beds each... Mr T., a devoted City Missionary... read about the Good Shepherd, and then made a few apt and racy comments, closing with the benediction, and a cheery, "Good night, friends ..."... If the London City Mission had done nothing more than this work ... it would deserve high honour and loyal support.'*

City missionaries were no respecters of rank. They knew that rich and poor had equal need of the gospel of salvation through Jesus Christ. But they also knew that the rich were within reach of the church, while the poorest of the poor were neither reached by parish churches nor would they always be welcome should they decide to go into them. Consequently, missionaries tended to work within the lower classes of society and those who had dropped out of society altogether.

When, in 1889, the Metropolitan Board was replaced by London County Council, the Housing of the Working Classes Act the following year paved the way for the demolition of the worst slum property and the building of houses close at hand to accommodate those who had been evicted. From then until the outbreak of World War I there was a vast programme of inner-city regeneration. Numerous slums were torn down and blocks of flats built to replace them. Croydon, Deptford and Brixton were among the areas redeveloped at that time. The sad fact was that the rents of the new houses were often beyond the means of the people for whom they were intended. In one area, where 5,719 people were evicted to build housing for 5,500, only 11 of the original tenants moved into the new LCC blocks. The remainder went from their slums to others as bad or worse in a different part of the city. And the missionaries, as always, went with the people, whether to council estate or slum. Unlike parish churches, that can find themselves isolated in depopulated areas, missionaries move with their people and continue their ministry to them.

Reversed to vanishing point

The circumstances of the very poor changed little over the years. In 1948 Joseph Currie, missionary, wrote an account of a visit to a lodging house that could have come right out of the previous century. *'I came across an aged lodger sitting without socks or shoes ... His socks he had worn heel to toe and toe to heel until they lacked both. I should explain that when the toes of socks have been worn beyond repair one can (if one must) reverse the socks, so that the heel holds the toes and the place where the toes once nestled then flaps under the instep. This robs the leg of some of its length, but one cannot have it three ways unless the socks are quite whole. My aged friend had "reversed" so often that the socks had completely vanished. ... I wrapped my scarf around his feet to keep them warm, then I prayed with the old man and promised to try and find footwear for him. On my way home I purchased second-hand shoes from a dealer ... I had no difficulty about the socks for a Christian lady had knitted some pairs of socks, put a half-crown and a gospel booklet in the leg of each, and sent them to my Mission headquarters.'* Currie returned to the lodging house late at night and delivered his gifts. The old man, *'gave a smile as he said, "I'll just have to take them off again, but they will be quite safe. I'll put a shoe under each leg of my bed, and then when I lie on my bed they will be pinioned to the floor. No-one could steal them without lifting the bed, so they will be quite safe.'*

Much has changed in London since Joseph Currie was a missionary, but some things are the same. The city still has its homeless population: young people who came looking for streets paved with gold and who now sleep on the pavements, others for whom homelessness is a life-style option; and hundreds who have psychological and psychiatric problems. The policy of 'care in the community' has meant that an increasing number of those who find difficulty coping with life find themselves homeless in the capital.

The LCM still has a concern for the homeless and works among them. Faced with the physical, mental and social problems which characterise many of these people, missionaries believe that a meaningful encounter with Jesus Christ is the most effective way to a profound and lasting change of lifestyle. The words that missionaries speak and the practical caring and friendship they provide, all serve to underline the reality and relevance of the Saviour.

8

The Daily Round of a City Missionary

'*Missionaries often remain for many years on their beat, and, becoming well known and being honest kindly people, their periodical visits are welcomed. It is their duty to "put in a word for Christ", and they have no other duty than that described in this simple way. The rules of the Society forbid almsgiving, and the relations of the missionaries with the poor are by this made all the better... The place these missionaries fill and the part they play are quite unique: their experiences are related with the conviction and naivety of a medieval saint. Not too far removed in social status from those they visit — father confessor at once and friend; themselves absolutely satisfied of the truth and sufficiency of the simple Gospel they preach; neither distrusted nor pandered to; ...with a good word for every Evangelical Church or Protestant sect — they are, more than all the rest, in tune with the sentiments of the people.'*
Charles Booth, *Life and Labour of the People in London*, 1902

'*I am more than ever convinced that..the backbone of mission work is visit, visit; and then begin again and visit consecutively. With all our open air and Mission hall work, marching and parading the streets and courts of my district, the only real, vital way to reach them is to visit them single-handed.'*
City Missionary in South London, 1896

'...we find London dotted over with (mission halls of various sorts)...In the poorer parts especially, in almost every street, there is a mission; they are more numerous than schools or churches, and only less numerous than public-houses. The whole of this work, Church of England, Nonconformist, or unattached, is interwoven with that of the Society known as the "London City Mission"....The primary object of this remarkable organisation is the spread of the Gospel by systematic house to house visitation; but the Society seeks to combine its work as far as possible with that of others in the same field...'
Charles Booth, 1902

'It is now twenty-four years since I was privileged to go to Bethnal Green, and I am thankful that I can look back and, by the grace of God, say that I fully believe that over 200 people have been soundly converted to God there. I never saw trade so bad (as it is now), employment so hard to obtain, and so many men out of work. "No food, no money" is the cry on every hand ... I fed them on bread, jam, and tea, and never did I see men eat like them.'
Missionary Henry Lockyer, 1904

Sixty years into its ministry, the London City Mission's work was well established and had developed a routine of its own. While 53 of the 500 missionaries in 1890 were engaged in meeting workers at their places of employment, most were following Nasmith's original vision as they tramped the streets and alleyways of their districts, knocking on door after door for week after week and year after year. To understand the life of a missionary, what better than to walk around his district with him. Henry Lockyer was appointed to Bethnal Green in 1880 and contemporary records paint a bleak picture of the sights, sounds and smells with which he would have been all too familiar.

'*The houses are always much crowded. Lately, many have become overcrowded in consequence of the pulling down of small houses for the erection of artisans' dwellings. I believe within twelve months the number of families living in my district will be largely increased. When Pepys wrote his Diary, giving an account of the Fire of London, he said, "Having housed my possessions in the remote village of Bethnal Green, I returned to London to see after the Admiralty papers." My district must then have been a pretty rural spot. The most wretched amongst the present houses were once rows of pretty village cottages of one or two stories, having large pieces of garden-ground in front and rear. This ground is now covered with ill-drained, dirty sheds, used by costermongers for various purposes. Time has brought the remote village of Bethnal Green within the very heart of London ... During the inclement weather of last winter the poor in my district suffered great hardships. Thirty-eight inquests were held in the East of London on the bodies of persons who died of starvation. When I have seen the dear children with pinched faces, blue with cold, and with scarcely anything to cover them by day or by night, I have lifted my heart to God on their behalf, and, glory be to his most holy Name, He has brought my desires to pass. During the winter 17,340 free breakfasts were given to poor* children, besides free teas and suppers both for adults and children living in my district. Also, 1,019 pairs of boots, about 800 suits of clothes, and flannel and calico garments were distributed among the poor.'

Missionaries were required to keep a record of their work in Journals that were submitted on a regular basis to the LCM Headquarters for inspection. Few of the 19th Century Journals have survived, but one of Lockyer's has. It enables us to step into the shoes of a London City Missionary for the month of June 1895, as we read it exactly as he wrote it:

2nd June
After Tea conducted the Service in the Chapel & had a fair attendance. Afterwards my Workers and I went & helped Bro. Robins conduct an Open Air Service on his district till 10pm. It was a good meeting many men being in heart dealt with Personally.

Monday 3rd
I did not do any visiting today as it was Whit Monday. But in the Afternoon I took my Band of Workers to Wanstead Flats to take part in an Open Air Service with Mr. Boston. It was a very good meeting, one man being under conviction of sin decided for Christ.

Tuesday 4th
To day I held my Anniverssary of the Boys Lodge by having an excursion to Chingford. & 68 availed themselves of the treat.

Wednesday 5th
Holiday

Thursday 6th
George Gardens. I began my consecutive visitation of these gardens.

No1 I here met Mr. & Mrs. Lythgo & their family just returned home from work. My heart was filled with joy at knowing that this family has been blessed through the missionary's visit, 5 of them having confessed conversion to God. We had a profitable conversation on different parts of the Bible. Instead of having our usual Service in the Hall we took the Harmonium & went to the Top of the Rd & held an Open Air Service till 10.

Friday 7th
George Gardens. To day I returned to my consecutive visitation of these gardens & talked to the people at their doors & in their homes. But nothing of special interest came out of it But spiritual exhortation and hearing their many troubles.

Saturday 8th
I did not do any visitation to day as it is not convenient for the people. So I prepared for the coming day.

Sunday 9th
I did not attend any place of Worship this morning as I gave my wife that priviledge & I looked after the little ones. In the afternoon I opened my hall for the school & had a good attendance of Scholars and Teachers. After school we had an Open Air Service on the district & it was cheering to see so many men come out of their cottages & listen to the reading of God 's Word. After Tea in the hall we opened the hall for our usual Service & I was glad to see so many present as it was very hot. But I am thankful to say that our meetings are well sustained by young people and some are being passed on into Church Fellowship. After this Service we went to the top of Old Bethnal Gr Rd & held an Open Air Service till 10pm & this was an encouraging Service for we could see tears running down the cheeks of many.

Monday 10th

I did not visit consecutively to day as so many of the people are running to the Pawn Shop with the Sunday Clothes so I visited some of the sick & the afflicted.

Canrobert Street. 26. I here met Mr. & Mrs. Tranter both of them ill. Mr. Tranter has just had one eye taken out and is losing the sight of the other. Mrs. Tranter is suffering from Asthma. I found by conversation that they were very good people & had lived a moral life, attending a place of Worship when they could and in this they were trusting. But from the Word & many illustrations I led them to see their need of the precious Blood and after a word of prayer I left them feeling that I had not called in vain.

At 7 o'clock I opened the hall for the Lad's Meeting. But the light night's & the hot hall keep's many away and tonight we did not have many. At 8.15 we held our Men's meeting But not many present. We also conducted an Open Air Service in the Hackney Rd & a good number stood & listened till 10.15 & most of them were men enjoying their pipe.

Tuesday 11th

George Gardens. This morning I returned to my consecutive visitation of the gardens. 30 I here met Mrs. Simms who was very much agitated, she buried a little one some time ago & some ignorant people have been telling her that it cannot enter the kingdom of heaven because it was not Baptized & the Scripture Reader had called & when asked the question replied, 'That is a serious question and one we must leave with God.' What do you think Missionary? Your little one is in Heaven as you sit there. I confirmed what I said by quoting the text, 'Behold the Lamb of God that taketh away the sin of the World' & I believe that sin was the sin we inherit from our parents & every child goes to heaven because of the death of Christ and they are not judged by God & held responsible until they come to a knowledge of the law and break it. I quoted the Words of David when his Child died, 'I shall go to him.' And she was comforted with the thought that trusting in the Lord Jesus she would see her loved one again. Mothers Meeting in the Afternoon again with a good number present.

Wednesday and Thursday 12th and 13th
George Gardens. I resumed my consecutive visitation these two days & called upon 42 families. They all treat me kindly & some admit me into their homes on purpose for religious conversation & others stand at their door. But for all of them the message of Redeeming love is put before them for their acceptance. This Evening I did not hold my usual Service in the hall But took the Harmonium out to the corner of the street & we had a good number stop & listen.

Friday 14th
Annual Communion Service.

Saturday 15th
I did not do any visitation to day as it is not convenient for the people. Men are finishing their work to take home & women are finishing their Washing & cleaning the house.

Sunday 16th
I did not attend any place of Worship this morning but gave my wife the privilege.

At 2 oclock I opened the hall for the school but did not have so many present as usual as it was very hot & the Boys get away into the park. After School we went into a Blind Court in Middle Walk & held an Open Air Service till 5 & the people hear the Word of God as I read it myself as loud and plain as I possibly can. At 6.30 I opened the hall for our usual Service & it was a good meeting. Tonight I gave the young Converts the priviledge of testifying what the Lord had done for them & it made a good impression upon the older ones. After the Service we went again into the Open Air & held a Service until 10.15.

Monday 17th

I did not visit consecutively to day, But made special calls to the sick.

George Gardens. 40 I here met Mrs. Law who is suffering from Bronchitis. I have visited this family for 15 years & I am thankful to say not in vain. She is now trusting in the Lord Jesus as her Saviour & now attend's the house of God regularly. Her eldest son died some time ago having been converted through listening to the Gospel in the Open Air. Temperance Work as usual & an Open Air Service in Hackney Rd.

Tuesday 18th

Bethnal Gr Rd. This morning I visited the Dispensary Shops, & Whitmores Granary. At the granary the men are very rough But I was enabled on one of the floors to put the gospel before one Man & point him to Christ. Mothers Meeting at 2 o'clock with a good number of low Women present from the district. Many of these women do not attend any place of Worship & would not this one if there was not a clothing club attached to it.

At 8 we have the Christian Band with a good number present.

Wednesday 19th

Shay Bulb Factory Shoreditch. To day I visited a part of this factory which is grown from 60 to 300 & to day I done the Men & part of the Women & I was cheered on visiting the men to find that two young men have just been converted in one of our Mission Halls in Hackney Rd and were letting their light shine amongst their mates amidst persecution. At 8 o'clock we opened our hall for the rough children of the St and it was a sight to see them as the gospel was put before them. At 9 Mutual Improvement Class.

17th June
Thursday Friday
George Gardens. I resumed & finished my consecutive visiting of these gardens. But nothing of special interest came out of it But tract distribution & spiritual exhortation to the people.

Saturday 22nd
I did not visit to day But prepared for the coming day.

Sunday 23rd
I did not attend any place of Worship but gave my wife the priviledge of doing so. At Two Oclock I opened the hall for the school and had a fair attendance of children and teachers. After School we went & held an open air service in George Walk till 5. After Tea we opened the hall for our usual gospel service & it was a good time of decision. After the Service we went again into the open air till 10 & a lot of men & women going home from their day's pleasure stop for a few minutes and listen to the gospel.

Monday 24th
I did not visit consecutively to day But visited some of the sick & afflicted.
    25 Mansford St. I here met Mr. Mortimer who is Blind & his wife is suffering from Chronic Bronchitis & Rhumatism & to day she was suffering much. But they have much reason to thank God for sickness for it was through having a sick child the Missionary called and now 7 of them through the Missionarys effort are converted to God and are in Church fellowship Well may the old man continually say, 'God Bless the L. C. Mission.' Temperance Work as usual & an Open Air Service in Hackney Rd.

Tuesday 25th
Old Bethnal Gr Rd. To day I visited this Rd & all the people seemed willing to listen.

Chandler shop — I here met Mr. Hitchcock who wants to feel before he's converted what the christians talk about of peace & joy. Gas Fitter's Shop — Mrs. Bullock say she knows what I say is true but she can't give up the drink. Plumber's Shop — Mr. & Mrs. Abbey are both church people & did believe in the high doctrine I brought before them, 'Except ye be converted & become as little children ye cannot enter the kingdom of heaven.' Mothers Meeting as usual in the Afternoon and Christian Band in the Evening.

Wednesday, Thursday & Friday
These three days I visited over 50 families in Middle Walk putting the gospel before them at their doors & in their homes.

Saturday
I did not visit but prepared for the services of the Sunday.

Sunday 30th
I did not attend any place of Worship this morning but gave my wife the privilege.

In the Afternoon I opened the hall for the School & had a good attendance of children & Teachers & a good work is going on in the Senior Class.   Open Air as usual in the Gardens & I was pleased to see so many Men stand in their gardens & listen to the Word of God. At 7 we held our usual Service & I had some strangers in our midst and the Word was with power. After the service we went to the top of the road and held a meeting till 10 and it was a good time.

What strikes the reader of Lockyer's journal is the patience of the man as he faithfully visited his district, looking for opportunities to share God's Word. He did have his encouragements, and we can feel his joy as he notes them, but for every encouragement there seemed to be dozens of rejections. But what is even more striking is that in another surviving Journal that he wrote ten years later, we find him still plodding the same streets, still knocking the same doors, and still prayerfully looking for opportunities. No doubt Henry Lockyer was encouraged in his labours by his Superintendent and the staff at the LCM Headquarters, but God alone knew the hundreds of miles tramped, the thousands of doors knocked, and the countless hours prayed for the people of Bethnal Green where he worked for no less than 48 years, from 1880 to 1928.

9

The Life and Times
of a City Missionary

'It is my belief, Watson, founded upon my experience, that the lowest and vilest alleys of London do not present a more dreadful record of sin than does the smiling and beautiful countryside.'
'Sherlock Holmes', 1892

'The City missionaries find visiting very hard in a new district. Another missionary says he would rather visit men than women; he can get something out of them. "They will say what they think when they don't agree, whereas with women it is 'Yes, sir'— 'No, sir'— and 'Good day', and all over when the door is closed."'
Charles Booth, 1902

'The question how to get at London is always present. The mission services do not attract those for whom they are meant, but rather those who have been to church or chapel elsewhere, or such as prefer a free and easy meeting to a regular service. They do not bring the poor from the slums; to these the Gospel must be taken.'
A Church of England clergyman, 1902

'In a number of locales, young men formed "Skeleton Armies" to pursue Salvation Army processions; they mocked and often attacked the Salvationists....Other missionary societies, like...the London City Mission, instructed their brethren to go quietly among the people and to avoid arousing a commotion in order to win the trust and confidence of the unredeemed. Occasionally these evangelists did

meet with ridicule or opposition, but they did not count it in their
favour. Salvationists expected to rouse the devil and infuriate sinners.'
Pamela J. Walker, *Pulling the Devil's Kingdom Down,* 2001

'Some years ago I made an awful mistake — I tried to be a parson.
Finding out (my) mistake, "I said 'I have had enough of that; I will
just be a natural man in a natural way; I will go and speak to the
people in the most simple way I can, and talk to them in their own
language."'
City Missionary, John Davis, 1894

'In the afternoon I made calls at twenty-one homes and found serious
trouble in nineteen of them, trouble in connection with which I did
not seem to be able to give either help or comfort.'
John Galt, 1890s

'The work to which I was appointed was that of evangelising the
cabmen of London ... the problem was how to handle those reputedly
keenest men in the world in matters of argument and repartee. First
experiences seemed to indicate that the half had never been told so
far as the keenness and ready wit of London cabmen was concerned.
At every cab-rank it appeared that there was a man ready and waiting.'
John Galt, 1898

Henry Lockyer's journal gives us a snapshot of the daily routine of a district missionary at the end of the 19th Century. Other missionaries wrote more widely and in more detail about their lives. Notable among these was John Galt, who served in the LCM for 17 years from 1890. Late in life he wrote a remarkable, but unpublished, autobiography that gives us a vivid account of a missionary's life.

A single to London

John was born in 1863 near Elgin, in the north of Scotland. His home was poor and became poorer over the course of his childhood. But it was a literate home and, because the boy had an enquiring mind, he read all he could get his hands on. When, aged 21, John moved to London he had been a Christian for three years. Within a few days of arriving in the city, two things happened to him: he was challenged regarding missionary service and he found work in a drapery firm. The first outlet for his missionary zeal was with a little group from his church that took services in a local common-lodging house. Drapery would seem an innocuous business, but when the January sales arrived, John had a problem – the sales tickets were full of untruths. Cheap stock bought in especially for the sales was advertised as being dramatically reduced. Unable to lie, he handed in his notice. His next job involved staying in a men's hostel and sharing a room with four others. An incident there illustrates his ability to state a strongly held view in an inoffensive way. A bottle of whisky was being handed round to celebrate a birthday. Declining the offered drink, Galt, instead of preaching his temperance principles, told his room-mates, *'All of you must know by this time that I have no more brains than I need for immediate use every hour of the day and that I couldn't do with any less.'*

Before many months had passed, John Galt's minister, the well-known F.B. Meyer, encouraged him into full-time service with a London church whose congregation was dwindling. His job was to visit the homes and common-lodging houses around the church, speaking to people about Jesus and inviting them to attend services. He worked under the auspices of the 'Forward Movement'. With a band of young men, he held 'Gospel singsongs' in the various lodging houses. '*Thus,*' he says, '*was the work of taking the gospel to the submerged of the district begun.*' Mission Bands of both men and women made quite an impact on the community, with hardened souls being softened by grace. While some such bands were made up of refined young people, Galt's group were from working-class backgrounds and had no social pretensions. This opened his eyes to the effectiveness of ordinary people reaching ordinary people for Jesus.

In at the deep end

What prompted Galt's application to the London City Mission, was the suggestion that he continue with the work he was doing by joining the LCM, with the Forward Movement contributing half of his salary. He was accepted, but it came as a surprise when, at the end of his training period, he was appointed, not to his old area, but to Tent Street in Bethnal Green where the missionary had just retired on health grounds. John's previous experience made him an obvious choice. Soul-searching soon gave way to submission, and the following Sunday he met for the first time a hall packed full of children in Tent Street. '*A worker was commanding and beseeching silence and order,*' he commented, '*and getting neither. Presently he bethought him the expedient of shouting, "This is the new missionary." Fourteen teachers were present and they seconded the efforts of the man on the platform by shouting at the pitch of their voices for silence and enforcing their commands with sundry and divers boxings of ears and dire threats if the scholars did not "Hold their row."'* The racket heralded John Galt's appointment as a London city missionary.

The condition of the people among whom he worked was pitiful. *'Poverty, deep and grinding and continuous was the rule and even a moderate measure of plenty or comfort the exception. An overwhelming majority were ill fed, ill clad and worse housed. The standard meal of the women and children was bread, hot from the bakers oven, with a smear of margarine, plum jam or pease pudding by way of relish. Much of the clothing of the people was bought second hand at very low prices from wardrobe dealers who plied their trade in the gutter of the market streets. Boots and shoes were bought from the re-makers who mended one old shoe with the materials taken from another one too old to be repaired and the price ranged from 1/- up. The average frontage of the dwelling measured eleven feet six inches so the rooms were very small yet the rents counted per cubic foot of space were about four times greater than that of the houses of, say, Belgravia. This being so, a minimum of space per family was aimed at resulting in dense overcrowding, and the prevalence of insect pests.'*

These poor homes were also workshops, as most of the women were engaged in 'sweat work' of some description. One told the new missionary that they were, *'Driving life out to keep it in at this here sweat work.'* While the women in the district made matchboxes, trousers, bird cages, brooms, shoes and even furniture, the men were mostly casual labourers.

Less than half the population of Bethnal Green was literate and Galt reckoned that the people were, in the main, ignorant of even the basics of the Christian faith. The common perception seems to have been that entrance to the kingdom of heaven depended on getting a clergyman to a deathbed before the dying person breathed his last. When telling the missionary of a middle of the night dash with a minister to her mother's death-bed, the teller concluded, *'Didn't we think it lucky that we got 'im in time for if we hadn't mother might be in the place down below for ever an' ever. She was a pretty rough un wuz mother.'*

John Galt considered the situation in which these poor people found themselves and concluded that their money was being spent on drink and gambling, the drink to give a temporary feeling of wellbeing and the gambling to provide a quick thrill and the possibility of a better tomorrow. He had 1,100 people in his district and he walked the streets and knocked the doors five hours daily, talking to them of the man Jesus, who had known hardship and ill treatment, and who could sympathise with their needy situations. But for all his strenuous efforts the numbers attending the Mission Hall diminished alarmingly. This was due partly to their affection for his predecessor, and partly to the fact that the previous missionary had wealthy friends who passed on financial help for needy people whereas Galt had, as yet, no-one to whom he could go for such assistance.

The final straw

Things came to a head when the young people boycotted his ministry because he had stopped their Fife and Drum Band. What they didn't know was that the instruments, which had not been paid for, had been returned to their rightful owner by the previous missionary before he left! So incensed were the young folk that they threw bricks against the hall's swing doors and pelted worshippers with mud. Perhaps it is not surprising that attendances dropped from 150 to 20–40 within six months. But they reckoned without Galt's ingenuity. Having discovered that a feature of his predecessor's ministry had been an annual excursion, he set out to plan the biggest and best one yet, drip-feeding the people with information about it as the date drew nearer. When the great day came, 14 large horse-drawn waggons started from the Mission Hall, all loaded to the limit with young and old. Paper flags waved, horns tooted and penny whips cracked. Most of the lads who had boycotted the meetings stripped to the waist and ran alongside.

But the excursion was a nine-day wonder, and before long things were even worse than before. The situation began to get Galt down. It was when he reached his lowest point that God intervened to encourage him. '*A manilla envelope with a halfpenny stamp, probably another circular! But no, the postmark showed that it came from my home town. It contained a small card with plain printing, the name of the minister and a verse of poetry which read thus:*

> *Thou art as much His care as if beside,*
> *Not man nor angel lived in heaven or earth;*
> *The sun alike pours forth his glorious tide,*
> *To light up worlds or wake an insect's mirth.*

Reading the lines I became aware of my having questioned the care and kindness of God and that the God whose care I had questioned had, the while, been planning and timing for me, in spite of my guilt of unbelief.' That solved his personal problem, but not his professional one, though it brought it to a head. He decided to go to God with a test: if the attendance at the next prayer meeting was decidedly greater than usual, or if there were signs that it was especially blessed, he would take it as God's will he should continue. If not, he would resign. Five minutes before the next prayer meeting, not even the caretaker was there. The only person in sight was a lad who was doing some repair work in the hall. But by the end of the evening, the lad was a Christian and the group gathered in the hall was bigger than usual. John Galt stayed.

It would be nice to record that from then on things were very different, but Galt lived in the real world. The difference was that he was no longer alone, and he was sure that the new convert would be the key to the lads, and that the lads would be the key to his ministry. As winter came on, he saw the young troublemakers huddling together for warmth. *'I've got a great idea,'* he told his ally. *'Have you really ...'* the young man replied. *'I would stick to it if I were you, you might never have another.'* And that's what Galt did. His idea was to do good to those who were harming the cause, and he did it by lighting a fire in the Mission Hall on cold evenings and letting the lads come in and get warm on the promise of good behaviour and that they would listen to a three minute talk. The fire was lit, and within weeks the first of the boys was converted. He was not the last, though there were some others who went from bad to worse. One of them was eventually hanged as a murderer, despite Galt writing to the Home Secretary for clemency.

The fire-side gatherings began towards the end of his second year in Bethnal Green, and were a real breakthrough. But disappointment followed quickly when the Mission Hall lease came up for renewal at a rent that was thought by Headquarters to be too high, and the owner of the hall's furniture demanded it back. The decision was taken to close Galt's hall and to transfer him to Poplar. He records that, *'Dismay followed the announcement of the closing order and the removal of the missionary to another field of labour. All the workers and young converts pledged themselves to seek affiliation with some church or mission and to keep on working and these pledges were kept to the letter.'*

In Bethnal Green Galt had used *Horner's Penny Stories* in his evangelism, and he continued to do so in Poplar, effectively setting up a lending library. 'That', he comments, 'was the work of the girls and women.' The men of his new Mission Hall distributed the *Christian Herald* in public houses. Very soon he was *'on speaking terms with every landlord ... and on nodding terms with almost all the men in the community.'* Galt's industry is clear from his fourth Poplar Annual Report, which shows that *'sixty thousand book exchanges had been made, nine hundred and fifty gospel meetings held, over a mile of one grade of flannelette had been sold and made into garments at the mother's meeting, and five tons of literature with a definite Christian content had been distributed, the bulk of the latter being Christian Herald back numbers. The number of tracts distributed in the workhouse, in the shops in the East India docks and elsewhere ... at least fifty thousand.'*

The Great Hunger

In November 1893, John Galt married Miss Francis, who had come from F.B. Meyer's church to help with the Bethnal Green Mothers' Meeting. And it was not long before they were facing a terrible challenge. The winter of 1894 became known as the Great Hunger, and the people of Poplar suffered terribly. Galt tells the story movingly. *'My wife and I distributed two tons of bread in about three weeks ... when all the available money we had was 14/9. ... The Thames was frozen over so that drays were crossing on the ice at Blackwall and elsewhere and not one ship came up or went down the river for nearly two months. The people dependent on the shipping docks and shipyards were starving; everything was pawned that could be pawned. Funds were being raised and distributed with which to feed the starving but although I was right in the midst of the distressed area in Poplar I was overlooked. I suppose that somehow it* was known that I had a friend who was able, and as willing as able, to help out in any emergency but it was not known that my friend was at that time on a tour round the world ... We were at our wits' end for people were coming to our door all day long, asking for help and we were at the end of available means.'

In one freezing cold home '...two small boys had their feet tied up in rags and were crouching close together on a palliasse for the sake of the mutual warmth of their bodies. In the mother's lap lay a baby, the only member of the family getting regular meals. But even the baby was so thinly clad that the mother tried to cover it with her bare arms while it cried from cold. The man had been out looking for work for days and getting none. He now was at the point of collapse.'

'Convinced that it could not be according to the will of God to say simply, "Be ye warmed and be ye fed," I went home to talk things over with my wife. The result was that we agreed to devote all the spare money we had, which amounted to 14/9, to buying bread, meanwhile taking the problem to God in prayer. Our belief was that He would make it possible for us to do just what He desired should be done. So fifty loaves were ordered and fifty cards issued to cases of extreme need, during that afternoon as I visited. During my absence my wife wrote four letters to friends ... in these she told how the people were placed ... but nothing was asked for...'

'The following morning while at breakfast the postman brought two letters in answer to those sent the day before. They contained money orders for 15/-, 3d more than we had expended for bread. When we arrived at the Mission Hall we told the assembled people how we had shared with them in providing a loaf for each family but that we had no more money of our own to give. God had, however, heard and answered our prayers on their behalf. ... That afternoon I issued 25 more cards and the next morning letters came to hand with sufficient cash to pay for the bread. Day after day we increased the number of cards issued and day after day the larger amounts received *were found to be sufficient. This continued for nearly three weeks although no more letters were written. One day in the third week the lady who had been one of the two who responded on the first day wrote again. She said in this her second letter that she had been reading about the distress in Poplar and had become ashamed of the contribution she had sent and had pleasure in enclosing double the first amount. There was, however, no enclosure so we decided to wait a whole day to give the lady time to discover her mistake. Next day she wrote again saying that when she discovered the mistake ... she mentioned it to her husband and their son-in-law. Her husband asked her how much she was sending and on being told made fun of the smallness of the amount. She retaliated by asking how much he was going to give and she had pleasure in enclosing two cheques from the men of the house, one for two guineas and one for one guinea. We received no more donations but that money enabled us to feed the hungry till the very day when every man who could stand up had a job waiting for him.'*

It was little wonder that his exertions began to tell on John Galt's health, and he was sent away for some weeks rest. What he found on his return was disturbing. Older workers had given advice to younger ones, possibly without much tact, and the advice was resented. Complaints were made by both parties; but, in spite of every effort made, harmony was not completely restored. After discussions at Headquarters, it was decided to move Galt to a new district. *'It was announced and instantly peace smiled her blessing once more.'* It was obviously the right time to go.

Moving on

Galt's third LCM posting was to the cabmen of a large sector of the city. For the following nine years he walked his district, speaking to cabmen, helping them with their problems and trying to answer their difficult questions. Cabmen then, as now, are the philosophers of London, and more than willing to engage in discussion. Galt, with his sharp mind and quick wit, could have out-argued many of them. But he had some lessons to learn. *'It came about that what might be called the "words of men's wisdom" proved of little use in the work in which I found myself engaged. It seemed necessary and reasonable to depend on the promise that "It shall be given you in that same hour what ye shall speak."... Moreover it soon became clear that what one was able to tell of the things of God in their own experience had far greater effect than what one tried to prove by mere argument.'* It would be wrong to suggest that things always went Galt's way, and he gives several accounts when others got the better of him.

John Galt and his wife had seen God's provision for the needs of their poor people; but they were not immune to poverty themselves. The family's health had a crisis. Mrs Galt developed pneumonia, John was diagnosed with a serious heart complaint, their daughter caught measles then scarlet fever, and their little son also got measles, which was immediately followed by dysentery and then diphtheria. Not wanting to ask the London City Mission for help, the parents struggled on. They were at their very lowest point when F. B. Meyer unexpectedly sent a nurse to help them, and a cheque for £15 15/- arrived in the post for manuscripts of tracts that Galt had sent to a Christian publisher for consideration. His was no academic knowledge of God's ability to provide, it was the basis of his daily living.

In his ninth year as missionary to the cabmen, and seventeenth year of service with the LCM, his son's health became an issue again. Medical advice was that the child's best chance of a healthy life was a complete change of climate. Canada was strongly recommended. *'It would be ideal also for all of us in every way'*, Galt noted, *'a great country with a splendid educational system, a land of plenty with not even one poorhouse between the Atlantic and the Pacific.'* Resigning from the LCM in 1907, Galt with his wife and children headed for the New World. Having set up home in Northern Ontario, John Galt became a minister, firstly in Kingsville where the main industry was silver mining, and where one of the first men he met was from Bethnal Green! He ministered to several churches over the following decades, and eventually died in 1942, aged 79.

10

Imperial Heyday

'London is the epitome of our times, and the Rome of today.'
Ralph Waldo Emerson

'The day of small nations has long passed away. The day of Empires has come... The City of London — the clearing-house of the world.'
Joseph Chamberlain, 1904

In the Tabard Street area (Southwark) the death-rate between 1904 and 1908 was 36.8, as against 14.9 for the rest of London.

'The home churches think we have terribly trying experiences, many discomforts and much to endure. I fail to see these and contend that our position is vastly superior to the hard working City Missionary. Our brethren have had trying work and do it with a smile. Let us be done for ever with the cant about hardship, or, comparatively few, the trials of mission work when they cannot be compared to those of the home pastor or city missionary.'
James Chalmers, Missionary to New Guinea, where he was killed by tribesmen in 1901

'In Bermondsey Street one night, a big brewer's drayman tried to upset the (open-air) meeting and sang a foul song right in the missionary's face. He stopped speaking and they sang a hymn. While the singing proceeded, Mr Davis looked kindly at the big fellow and said, "Yes, God bless you; you too may be washed in the blood of the Lamb." On this the drayman seized hold of the missionary, dragged him into his house just opposite, shut and locked the door. Then he

*called to his wife, "Sarah, come here and kneel down." They knelt.
"Now, Mr Davis, pray for my poor black soul." Prayer was offered.
Soon the drayman began to cry to God for mercy, and in less than an
hour he was changed from a foul-mouthed, devil-driven sinner into
a child of God.'*

From *A Marvel of Mercy*, the life story of John Davis

*Asked why some converts, instead of moving on to join a local church,
keep coming to the Mission Hall meetings, an (anonymous) City
Missionary replied, 'I think there are two reasons. First, missionaries
are easier to understand than ministers; and second, missionaries are
more fun than ministers.'*

The words of *Rule Britannia*, by James Thomson, were published in 1714 to commemorate the accession of the House of Hanover, but they were probably never sung with such fervour as they were at the turn of the 20th century, when much of the map was pink, and men were prepared to fight to keep it that way. The Boer War was half-fought and soldiers were in training to go out to speed the victory. The London City Mission fought too; only it fought the battle for men's souls. Never is that battle such a clear-cut issue as when young men are going to war and the only certainty is that not all will return. In a few cases, gospel work was not only for the good of the men's souls, but actually saved their lives. '*Among the invalids proceeding home in the next hospital ship is Private James Williamson, of the Black Watch, a native of Montrose. He was struck by six bullets at Magersfontein. One bullet hit a Testament which was in his breast-pocket over the heart. The ball glanced off the Testament and passed through his left arm, which it broke. He thus owes his life to the possession of a copy of the Scriptures.*'

LCM missionaries were quick to accept every invitation that came their way to speak to the boys. When Captain Saville, a Christian officer in the Middlesex Regiment, requested a visit to his barracks where 1,000 men and 30 officers were preparing to leave for South Africa, a missionary collected enough Gospels to go round and spent four days distributing them and talking with the soldiers. Before he left, all the men had accepted his offer of a Gospel. Another missionary, who visited the Royal Artillery Reserve, had his own way of making his point when a soldier was less than keen to hear him out. '*While I was giving out the Gospel of St. John,*' he wrote, '*a big fine man opened the door for a conversation, by saying it was no use bothering myself over them, as no one could be religious in this place. By way of arresting him, I asked him his name and number. He said,*

119

"What for?" I replied, "Then I shall know if you are among the killed."
He threw up his hands in horror, and exclaimed, "For God's sake don't
look for me there. I am not ready for that." I said, "But now is your
time." "Ah," said he, "my old mother said that. She's just like you"
(meaning a Christian). "Well, then," said I, "just let your mother have
the joy of knowing that her son is saved by the grace of God." I urged
him to decide for Christ, and he seemed in a promising condition of
mind.' Desperate situations require the use of desperate
remedies.

Soldiers' Homes, which the mission had been running for
years, provided a comfortable atmosphere in which men could
relax out of the barracks. Run by volunteers, mostly women,
the Homes were very well used. Some of the soldiers were
just boys, and many of them were from the country and had
never been away from home before. The Homes not only
provided a motherly ear, services were held in them, and
soldiers were converted.

Overwhelmed by numbers

A letter written in 1900 by the missionary at Woolwich to the
LCM Headquarters reminds us that the traffic between the
United Kingdom and South Africa was a two-way affair. The
man was feeling hard pressed by the heavy responsibility he
felt for the soldiers in the barracks, so much so that he wrote
asking if it were possible to have help, even if on a temporary
basis. He was quite overwhelmed by numbers and constant
movement. Not only was there a standing garrison of 6,000
soldiers, but newly trained men were leaving every day to fight
in the Boer War and new recruits arriving to begin their training.
Consequently the barracks were always full and always
changing. That would have been more than enough for one
man, but there was also a military hospital with 21 large wards

and 16 temporary iron huts in the process of erection. Five hundred wounded soldiers had already arrived back from South Africa, and another 500 were to follow. He knew that the wounded, many of them horribly maimed and mutilated, were not going to be short-term patients. Not only that, his missionary mind told him that reaching these victims of war with the good news of the gospel of Jesus Christ would spread it far beyond Woolwich were any to believe and take it home with them. The LCM responded to his plea for help, and an experienced man was sent for three or four days a week.

Of course, not all of the men who volunteered for service in the war were strangers to the gospel. Some had been regular in their attendance at church, and hundreds of them knew the work of the LCM well because they went to Mission Halls. Those missionaries whose work was centred in the halls were good to the men who left for the Cape, both in writing to them and in keeping those who attended their meetings praying for them. When the wounded were shipped home missionaries sought their own and ministered to them and their families. Among the heartbreaks of war there were real joys, such as a letter from one soldier in the Cape to a missionary who had cared for him. '*I was delighted to get a letter from you,*' the man wrote. '*I jumped with joy, that's a fact, as it took me back to old times.*' He went on to say that he had gone through such trials, troubles, difficulties and dangers he had never met before, living on half-rations for a time during a siege, and quarter-rations for a full three weeks. Yet, he assured his old friend, God had been with him. '*I long to see the dear old home again,*' the letter ended, '*and the meetings, and all kind friends; and the Lord will, I am sure, in His own time, allow me that privilege.*'

The end of an era

Then the Empire was shaken. At the beginning of 1901 Queen Victoria died. Although she was an old woman and not in good health, her death was sudden and unexpected. The Boer War was still raging, but it seemed as if the world had stopped. At its meeting on 28th January, the LCM's Committee wrote to the new king, Edward VII, assuring him of their prayers for his health, wisdom and grace.

Fifty years earlier, in 1851, when Victoria was just a young woman, she had watched as work began on the Crystal Palace in Hyde Park, probably the greatest ever symbol of British Imperialism. Had she been able to see what was happening at the site, she would have noted two LCM missionaries handing out an amazing total of 30,225 tracts to the workmen there. Supporters sent in gifts totalling £210 to ensure that visitors to the Great Exhibition in the new palace would be aware of a Christian presence. Immediately the Exhibition opened, eight missionaries positioned themselves on the roads leading to it, each with 2,000 tracts to distribute to visitors in the first week. Tracts were also available in a number of languages other than English. Besides distributing these, missionaries were instructed to get alongside people and speak to them on a personal basis. At least one took that literally. '*The more fully to identify myself with them, and the more freely to draw them into conversation, I sat down with those that sat, and was glad to lie down by others who, in idleness or from fatigue, indulged in that posture. By this means I met and conversed with the man that "never did nobody any harm,,"— with the sceptic, who admitted some and rejected other parts of the Bible, — with the Deist, who rejected all revelation as a cunningly-disguised fable, — with the scorning Atheist, who denied the existence of a God, — with the poor starving labourer out of work, and the idle vagrant, — with the outcast of the female sex, and with the most vicious of our own.'* He was a busy man for someone who spent part of his working day lying down!

Sunday observance

Prince Albert, the originator of the event, proclaimed it as, 'The Great Exhibition of the Industries of All Nations.' And so it was, but well over half of the 100,000 exhibits were from Britain and the British Empire. To the six million people who attended the Great Exhibition, set in the glass and cast iron magnificence of the Crystal Palace, it was the ultimate glorification of the British manufacturing industry. To none of this did London City Mission take exception. After all, it provided jobs for working people, took visitors from the city smoke to the clean air of Hyde Park where even the poor could enjoy the spectacle, and it offered an opportunity for mission. But there was an area of contention, and it was outlined in a formal letter to the Directors of the Great Exhibition. *'They* (LCM's Committee) *believe that the reported opening of the Palace on a portion of the Sunday would be – 1. A violation of the law of God. 2. That it would be a violation of the laws of the land, which could only escape public punishment by evasion. 3. That it would be most prejudicial to the religious and moral welfare of the working classes, adult and juvenile ... 4. That the evil effects to the immediate neighbourhood of the Palace ... would be a grievous infringement of the quiet of the Lord's-day, holding out a strong temptation to many of the inhabitants who now religiously observe that day to violate it. 5. That, on the numerous servants of the Palace and the Railway, a large amount of Sunday-work will be of necessity imposed.'* Having made its views known, the Committee recognised that the likely outcome was that an application would be made to Parliament to alter the law in favour of the new Palace. And that is what happened.

However, the LCM did not absent itself from the Crystal Palace because of Sunday opening. On the contrary, it even provided missionary services without the necessary funding being promised in advance as it saw the opportunities for spreading the Gospel to workers and visitors alike. As with all of the Mission's activities, there was a mixture of evangelism and pastoral work, and never was the pastoral aspect more needed than on Monday 15th July, 1853. The day began as normal and ended full of heartbreak. As one missionary was walking through the building, he heard the noise of falling timber and the screams of falling men. Suddenly the road was full of people, men and women running for their lives. From as much as a mile away the noise of crashing iron and glass could be heard. It took some time for the dust to clear and for a rescue effort to be safe. And when it was, the missionary was there to comfort as one mangled body after another was taken from under the wreckage and pronounced to be past hope or already dead. Try as he might, he could not gain the attention of the huddles of men, though the following day he could not meet the demand of those who wanted to speak to him or ask him for tracts. Ten men died in the tragedy.

Prince Albert's plan was that even the poorest would be able to visit his Great Exhibition, and they did in their hundreds of thousands. Rich and poor alike mingled among the stands, gaped at the inventions and gasped at the demonstrations. They saw things they had never imagined existed and went home intent on bringing their friends with them next time. The Crystal Palace was where to go and where to be seen. And it was also the place to meet the men from the Mission, although the results of their work were known only to God. The Committee noted that the nature of the work meant that it was impossible to report on its results as those who were engaged in conversation or received tracts often came from a distance. But it was content, on the basis of missionaries' reports, to leave the outcome in the Lord's hands. '*The day when there shall be emphatically the gathering together of all nations before the Judge of quick and dead will alone disclose the fruit which has resulted from the good seed of the kingdom so copiously scattered by the Mission at this memorable era in our great city's history.*'

A dome-shaped mission-field

Almost 150 years later, the Great Exhibition had a turn-of-the-millennium parallel in the controversial shape of the Millennium Dome. While it was still being built on the North Greenwich site, the LCM was approached with a view to providing missionaries as part of a Chaplaincy Team. Because the team was drawn from a wide range of churches it raised issues within the Mission, but it was decided to pursue the opportunity provided that the LCM's evangelical stance was not compromised. In the event, the LCM supplied four of the team of 20, three were active missionaries and the fourth worked at Headquarters. The team's remit was to be there for both staff and visitors. That was a considerable task, as between 4,000 and 5,000 people worked at the Dome and unknown thousands were expected to visit during 2000.

Part of the vast exhibition was set out as a Faith Zone, but the missionaries were not involved with that. Instead, they were given passes that allowed them to roam over the whole building (a space large enough to house 3,300 double-decker buses!), speaking to staff and visitors. The Chaplaincy Team had its base in a room designated as the Prayer Space. In theory, this was for people of every faith; in practice it was used only by those who associated themselves with Christianity. Each day of the year a short prayer service was held both morning and evening, and three services on Sundays. A book left in the Prayer Space, in which people were invited to write their prayer requests, was very well used. Over the course of the year seven books were filled, many asking for prayer for quite heart-rending situations.

LCM missionaries became more deeply involved with those who worked in the Dome than with visitors because they had the opportunity to get to know them better. Some extracts from a Dome missionary's diary – in which names have been changed – give a flavour of the work he did. '*I was pleasantly surprised to meet Ali while he was managing the queue for the Mind Zone. We met for a coffee and had a good chat. I also visited the Admissions and Ticketing Control Booth to let them know my schedule. I met Danielle as she was in the Admissions Booth for processing visitors paying by credit card. We had a very good conversation.*' '*I met Jacob later in the day and he will be taking a few days off to resolve some challenges he faces. He asks for prayer. I then met Flora. I noted she was not her usual bubbly self and she related a story of how her son died while on holiday in June. This was her first day back to work. She wrote a prayer in the Prayer Request Book. Her prayer reads. "Lord Jesus, I am back to work. Please help me be strong." I gave her a booklet on grieving and assured her of my/our prayers.*' '*I noticed a note in the Chaplain's Diary that Leon wanted to meet me today. I found him hosting the Rest Zone after searching for him through the Mind Zone. Please pray for him as he faces a particularly stressful situation he hopes to have resolved by this Monday.*' Christian staff were especially appreciative of the LCM's input, and for the support the missionaries were able to give them.

Between 1901 and 2000 the great empire of Queen Victoria vanished. But whatever pageantry and celebration are to be found in the streets and parks of London will continue to attract the presence and witness of City Missionaries.

11

Socialists and Revolutionaries

'The task of a City Missionary is to go where he is not wanted, until he is wanted.'
Lord Blythswood, 1911

'To say that I love my work is true, but it does not convey half the truth. I was never so happy as when I was amongst the men and I thoroughly enjoyed being with them. I know that in the greater number of instances this was reciprocated... What a fine body of men they are on the sailing barges! Robust, hearty and very healthy in appearance, a certain sailor-like carelessness that commends them to you... They hate all meanness and have a contempt for anyone who is not straightforward, but they also appreciate one who is faithful to his convictions, and has the courage to speak out, neither fearing the frown, nor courting the smiles of men.'
Edwin Blanchard, missionary to bargemen and canal boatmen, 1895 – 1923

'...in truth, the charitable relief given by the missions of almost every description is rarely wise. The dangers of overlapping are ignored, and the necessity for thoroughness, no less than for sympathy, is not grasped. The opinion, again of one of the Church of England clergy, that slums are over-visited and demoralised is held by many. We hear for instance of one poor street visited by about ten agencies, whose

combined efforts, it was said, enabled the people to live on charity, ...
and of the embarrassment caused by a large annual gift of dessicated
soup for which no use could be found.
 Charles Booth, 1902

London, 15th April 1912, *'First-day sales in excess of*
200,000 were claimed in London alone for a new national,
socialist newspaper, the Daily Herald.*' Its Editor said, "We*
know there is a real need for a first class socialist newspaper" .

'Carefully avoid all topics of an irritating tendency ...
Studiously avoid entering upon subjects of a political nature,
as altogether foreign to the purpose of your visit...'
The LCM Instructions to Missionaries

Leaders of the Mission in its early years

Missionary hounded out of a rookery

A court in the slums

Shovel-maker, Bethnal Green, c. 1890

Henry Lockyer (back row, cntre) in his early days at Bethnal
Green, (see chapter 8, pp. 91-101)

John Galt outside his mission-hall in Poplar, c. 1895
(see chapter 9, pp. 103-115)

Above: George Gillman (centre, rear) with Italian sailors, c. 1895

Missionary to 'Coalies' (left), with a portable harmonium (1899)

Charles Elgar (left), Missionary to Public Houses, Whitechapel, 1909.

LCM Day-School for Canal-boat children, Brentford, c. 1917

'Helping the Police with their enquiries' – Arthur Thomas, 1950

The Queen Mother opens the new LCM Headquarters, 1975

Bernard Hooper amid the tower blocks, 1970's

The 150th Annual Meetings, Royal Albert Hall, 1985

Daada Luogon, from Liberia, missionary in Kings Cross, 2000

Julie Piner (left), the first woman to be a LCM Missionary, 1989

Bush Hogg (right), at the centre of the homeless, Waterloo, 1993

On a winter morning in 1910 the City of London Police received word of a break-in at a jeweller's shop in Houndsditch. Within minutes three unarmed policemen were shot dead, along with one of the criminals who had been grabbed by the officers. The rest of the gang escaped, only to be cornered some days later at a house in Sidney Street, Whitechapel. Attempts to arrest them were repelled in a storm of gunfire, until the Home Secretary, the youthful Winston Churchill, ordered in soldiers from the Scots Guards who were stationed at the Tower of London. Churchill himself hurried to the scene, to supervise what became known as 'the siege of Sidney Street'. Eventually, three of the gunmen died in a blaze started by the soldiers' gunfire. Their leader, Peter Piaktow, escaped – to take a prominent part in the Bolshevik regime in Russia after the revolution of 1917. The gang were revolutionaries from Latvia, attempting to fund their activities by raiding the jeweller's shop.

The following Annual Report of the LCM commented severely on these events:

'It has been painfully brought home to the British public of late months, that a considerable number of Europe's off-scouring have taken advantage of England's traditional "open door", to settle in her large cities, and more especially in the far-spreading purlieus of the metropolis. Unfortunately, these alien criminals bring with them their debasing vices, their disregard for human or Divine authority, and their proclivity for murderous plottings and deeds...'

The 1913 Report returned to the theme. *'It must be remembered... that a by no means small proportion of (the) foreigners form a very undesirable element in our midst, being addicted to gambling and other vices (such as the practice of the terrible white slave trade), to anarchical plotting against authority, and to violent quarrellings amongst themselves...'* And these strictures were dramatically highlighted at that year's Annual Meetings when the Rev. Martin Anstey displayed a set of pistols, including a Mauser and a small revolver, together with boxes of Browning ammunition. He announced to the audience that these items had been *'handed over to one of the missionaries by a Russian anarchist who was happily converted on hearing the gospel for the first time'*. In the measured terms of the LCM Magazine, the display *'created a mild sensation'*!

That there were many anarchists and revolutionaries to be found in London around the turn of the century was well known. Writers such as Joseph Conrad and G. K. Chesterton described their lives and plots. Their activities helped to fuel a general reaction against granting asylum to refugees, a reaction that led to stricter laws being passed by Parliament. And, of course, it was no accident that 'a Russian anarchist' encountered a City missionary, for the revolutionaries were especially to be found in the poorer districts of the city where refugees and immigrants formed their own 'ghettos'. Visiting from door to door in Whitechapel and other East End districts inevitably produced such encounters.

Assassination!

In the West End they were not unknown either. In 1897, missionary George Gillman (whose work among Spanish- and Portuguese-speaking sailors in the docks was described in chapter 6) had noticed newspaper reports that the Spanish government was expelling 28 revolutionaries to England. When Gillman heard that these men had arrived in London he decided that it was his duty to search them out. Having tried, without success, to find them in Soho (where many foreigners settled) he later heard that they might be in the Tottenham Court Road area. He wandered up and down the back streets, seeing *'many shady characters'*, before he found a German hotel and discovered that the Spaniards were lodging there. Perhaps because he was thought to be a fellow-anarchist, he was allowed in and (in Spanish) greeted the men and said he had come on behalf of the Christians of London to offer advice and sympathy. But when he added that the great God had sympathy with all men, they launched into strong denunciation of all religion. Many of them had endured the tortures of the Inquisition in Barcelona and they regarded it as part of their duty to overthrow such religion. Sensing that further conversation was impossible, Gillman said that he would continue to pray for them. *'Don't do that,'* said one, *'We don't want your God's help. He did not give us any help when we suffered in prison, and we don't want it now.'* Another Spaniard said, *'We have been treated abominably, like brute beasts, but we will have our revenge on Canovas.'* Gillman left them, but the next week he saw on the newspaper placards 'Assassination of Canovas' — for, back in Spain, the Prime Minister had been shot. As a good missionary, Gillman *'went again and again and had further conversation with several'* of the men.

Eventually most of them moved on from London, and Gillman's assessment was that *'on the whole they were a bad lot'*. Yet two of them responded to Gillman's conversations and began attending Christian meetings. By the time they emigrated to Cuba one of them wrote to the missionary, *'I can truly say that Christ is my only hope. I read about him daily in the Bible. How happy am I in meeting with the Lamb of God, the only way of salvation.'* Another of the men later became the correspondent for a radical paper in Barcelona, and wrote most positively about his experiences in England. He even counselled his countrymen to give up their anarchism and to read the Bible so that they might enjoy *'the advantages of the workmen in England'*.

The abiding principle behind such work as Gillman's was expressed in the 1913 Annual Report: *'Much may, and probably will be done by way of legislation to safeguard the nation's interests; but the Christian Church should never forget that it has a duty to discharge towards these visitors to the shores of Great Britain, viz, to evangelise them, and thus, if possible, to transform them from agents of mischief into agents of blessing.'*

'Socialism'

From the London where Lenin and Stalin planned their revolution, to the present city with its exile groups and Islamic militants, LCM missionaries have continued to encounter foreign agitators. But, from its very beginning, the LCM also confronted 'subversive elements' from closer to home. The horrors of the French Revolution were still comparatively fresh in the public mind in 1835 and readily used to characterise all those who called for radical change in society. Until World War I these tended to be lumped together under the dread name of 'Socialists'. In 1839 that term referred particularly to the followers of Robert Owen, with his idealistic views of community and his rejection of Christian marriage. Such socialism developed into an ideology that abandoned the Christian belief in God and embraced free thought and materialism. Throughout the Victorian period 'Socialist Halls' were opened, with 'Socialist Sunday Schools' teaching anti-religious views. Some followers developed 'revolutionary socialism', adopting the violence of many of their continental (and especially Russian) colleagues. But the majority sought to achieve their goals by agitation, education, and political action. In addition, there was the whole movement of 'Christian Socialism', encouraged by some of the churches, and by no means necessarily *'opposed to Christian Truth'*, as an LCM publication of 1912 recognised.

Poverty and unrest

Whatever distinctions are recognised, however, the underlying problem of an impoverished and politically unrepresented population meant that City Missionaries frequently operated in a climate of unrest and agitation. An earlier chapter has described the great upheaval of 1848, the year of revolutions. In 1887 Trafalgar Square was occupied for several days by demonstrators who were eventually dispersed by troops and police in an event known as 'Bloody Sunday'. The funeral of some of that day's victims saw a massive demonstration of public support. The early years of the 20th century were marked by economic depression and widespread strikes, while the First World War was barely over before more strikes paralysed the city. Throughout the 1920s, economic instability and industrial unrest, culminating in the General Strike of 1926, fuelled expectations of a 'Bolshevik Revolution' in Britain, to imitate the one in Russia.

The LCM, though occasionally indulging in the too-common Christian practice of condemning such views from a safe distance, more often managed to get close enough to the people who held the views to enable conversations based on realistic understanding and genuine sympathy. Even the 'Lectures on Socialism' delivered in 1839 were intended for the ears of the Socialists themselves. The Mission tried to have the lectures delivered in a Socialist Hall, and invited Robert Owen himself to attend – which he duly did, being seated on the platform to hear the lecture entitled 'Is Marriage Worth Perpetuating?'!

Operating at street level as they did, the missionaries faced a wide range of 'socialist' objections to their message, from the unsophisticated to the carefully thought-out. Their answers revealed a similar range of Christian reactions. Speaking in the open air in 1895, during a period of strikes, a Bethnal Green missionary was challenged: *'Mister, don't your Bible say that we ought to do to others as we'd like to be done by? Why don't you go to capitalists and preach that doctrine to them; then perhaps they'd see the justice of sharing alike with the workmen?'* The missionary gave a detailed reply, describing how profit-sharing by employers and workmen had been tried in London as long ago as 1827, and again in the past 20 years, but had failed. *'Where do you get your information from, old man?'* the crowd asked. *'From Board of Trade returns'*, he replied. But when the missionary went on to add exhortation to his economic history, the crowd grew restive. He referred to a couple who *'were boozing on Saturday night until the houses closed'*. *'Ah! Hoo!'* the crowd jeered, *the old cry — 'You nasty, drunken working-men.'* Evidently the men were used to being told that their poverty and troubles were entirely due to their drinking habits, and thus their own fault. But (wisely or otherwise) the missionary was not to be put off his diatribe. *'I know men who spend quite half their earnings in drink. Is that money skilfully used? And are not these men largely the cause, through their abject poverty, of bringing trade to what it is in the district?'* This time the reaction was louder: several voices jeeringly answered, *'Hoo, Hoo, Hoo, the old grunt, "You nasty, drunken working-men."'* The missionary forged on, to speak of a true equality before God that is found through faith in Jesus, but one wonders how many of his audience were still listening.

Other missionaries in the same area took a different line. One attended local Socialist meetings for several weeks, simply listening to their speeches and complaints (these were reported at some length in an article in the LCM Magazine). When he was finally asked if he had anything to say to the socialists, he expressed sympathy with their poverty and suffering, but urged them to seek redress through lawful political activity rather than violence. The franchise was being extended, he reminded them, and the just demands of working men were no longer totally ignored. Then he, too, steered his address towards a clear presentation of the gospel, urging the men to seriously consider the claims and offers of Jesus Christ as the real remedy to individual needs and social ills.

Weaver the Socialist

Serving as missionary to cabmen in the early 1900s, John Galt wrote of his encounter with 'Weaver the Socialist' at the cabstand in Primrose Hill. Weaver believed that *'mankind was incurably good, only needing to be provided with opportunities for goodness instead of what is so generally provided — opportunities a-plenty for being bad!'* He then asked what Galt thought of his theory. *'I agree with your desire for a better social order,'* he said, *'and am glad to find that you not only think that there should be better conditions but feel that you ought to work to secure the same. As to mankind being incurably good, I must say that I disagree for the reason that I see no evidence that it is so. Even when God Himself set to work to give man ideal conditions, man found a way to be bad and to go wrong.'* 'But,' replied the socialist, *'one swallow does not make a summer, does it? Is it not an undeniable fact that if mankind is taken in the lump it responds to its environment and becomes like its conditions? Slum conditions produce slum people; vicious conditions produce vicious people, and so on it goes. You can't deny that, can you?'*

Perhaps neither man would have been aware that Weaver's argument was in some ways close to those used by the earlier City Missionaries, when they wrote of the terrible housing and sanitary conditions in the city, but Galt still denied the Socialist's absolute statement: *'Yes, I can deny that because I have for years been in personal touch with the people who have lived year in and year out in the very midst of what are known as slum conditions and I did not find them to be more vicious than those who live in the "Belgravias"...'* Galt adds with welcome honesty that although *'the above portion of dialogue may seem to favour the missionary's end of the argument it is undeniable that, throughout the discussion as a whole, the honours went to Weaver the Socialist up to the point at which he claimed that dependance on a "Problematical God" was a delusion and a snare and at best an opiate which caused many good and true men to be content with things as they are in the vain belief that at some other time and somewhere else wrongs would be righted and crooked things made straight. It ought to be "as plain as a pikestaff" that this is the place and the present is the time for righting things that need to be righted.'* When Galt mentioned Christians such as George Müller and William Quarrier (founders of orphanages) as evidence that God exists and that prayer is answered, Weaver was having none of it! *'It might be that such men were possessed of some mesmeric powers which made them able to influence others to co-operate with them and get things done'*, he said, and then added, *'You know, that although you are religious and believe all the things that these wonderful men believe, you cannot give instances from your own personal experience of God taking action outside the ordinary course of things. You have to tell of wonders that happened in other people's lives.'* Here at last Galt was on firmer ground, and was able to relate to Weaver how through prayer alone two tons of bread had been distributed to the starving people of Poplar (as described earlier, in chaper 9). At the end of the story, Weaver looked thoughtful for a minute, then he said, *'Well, I am prepared to admit that there are more things in heaven and earth than my philosophy has dreamed of. I mustn't say I don't believe you for I make it a principle not to doubt a man's word unless I have good reasons for doing so. I like that story, and I'll tell you what I'll do. I'll take you in my hansom to St. John's Wood* (cabmen's) *shelter if you will promise to tell that story to the men there.'*

Galt's conversation with Weaver included the common taunt, famously expressed by Karl Marx in 1848, that religion is *'the opiate of the people'*, a tool used by the wealthy to reduce the poor to impotent contentment with their lot. Yet, in the very year that Marx wrote 'The Communist Manifesto' a speaker at the LCM Annual Meetings had expressed and rejected the taunt. As recorded in an earlier chapter, the LCM was congratulated by many in that year of revolutions for helping to preserve London from an uprising similar to those which ravaged Paris, Berlin and Vienna. But no less a person than the Rev. Baptist Noel, a key figure in the founding of the Mission, stood up and carefully deflected the congratulation. *'Various speakers have adverted to the influence which the labours of this Society may have had in promoting the peace of this city, and preventing the shock ... from being more violent and from having more fatal effects. I fully concur that this Society has had a certain amount of influence in accomplishing that result ...But it would seem to me exceeding unhappy, and even, I should say, most fatal to this Society, if it were to be supposed that this was the object of our labours. The object of the labours of this Society is not to be a sort of subsidiary moral police, and to preserve the order of this community. There are many other excellent results which I believe follow the introduction of religion into any heart or family. It tends very much to restrain drunkenness; it turns the thief into an honest man; it would repress crime in all its branches; but these again are not the direct objects which this Society pursues. Nothing less is aimed at by the laborious missionaries ...than the salvation of those whom they address. They* wish to raise them, and to make them happy for time and for eternity...They wish to bring upon the families whom they visit all the comfort of the continual indwelling of the Holy Spirit. No less results than these would satisfy the benevolence of their hearts.' Noel went on to warn what would happen if the people on their districts thought that missionaries were there to try and keep the impoverished from rising up against the rich: 'if they thought that the missionaries went with a view to keep them in order, they would at once, instead of welcoming them as friends, be jealous of them as spies ... If it should be asserted among the Chartists or Socialists of this metropolis, that this Society exists ... because it wishes to teach the miserable to be content with misery and famine, while themselves (i.e. the leaders and supporters of the LCM) were supplied with all the comforts of life, it would steel the heart of every Chartist and Socialist against every missionary that might knock at his door. It is not, in fact, their object; and it ought not to be misapprehended by any of those to whom they go, that it is their object.'

Noel's words were still most relevant in the 1920s when London was wracked by the economic woes that followed the end of the World War I. The Russian Revolution was deeply feared by many, and as eagerly looked to by others. Bethnal Green became known as 'Red' Bethnal Green from the strength of local agitation and the desire of some on its Council to name a new housing estate after Lenin. Violence was in the air, with a missionary who toured Scotland in 1919 to raise support for the LCM reporting that the railway lines had been sabotaged by strikers at Perth, and that armed soldiers rode on the locomotive for the rest of the journey to Glasgow. The old epithet 'Socialist' was increasingly replaced by the new negative 'Bolshevik', as the Mission continued its ministry amidst the turmoils that culminated in the General Strike of 1926, when armoured cars appeared on the streets of London, troops guarded food convoys, and riots broke out in the East End. In Poplar, described as *'a storm centre, where the people were agitated and unnerved'*, the missionary continued with a series of evangelistic meetings, while workplace missionaries retained the respect and affection of the men sufficiently to hold meetings and address them even during the strikes. There was also turmoil in the docks, with many Indian sailors joining in the protests initiated in their homeland by Gandhi, protesting at British rule and the Amritsar massacre in 1919.

From Bolshevism to the LCM

Bolshevism was openly anti-Christian, and the missionaries faced frequent taunts as *'the tout of the Church and the tool of the Capitalist'*. But their work was not totally unsuccessful. During the 1920s at least two Bolshevik activists became City Missionaries, having been converted through the witness of the LCM. One was first reached when a missionary knocked on his door and addressed him as 'Brother'. Assuming him to be a fellow-communist, the man invited him in and launched into a diatribe on capitalism. The missionary reported: *'For one and a half hours I listened patiently, putting a word in here and there, without disclosing my errand or identity.'* Then the missionary's turn came. He spoke for a similar length of time about the Gospel! The Communist *'let off steam and reproached himself for being so short-sighted'*, but the missionary's message somehow impressed him deeply, and before his visitor left the house the man had made a commitment to Christ.

The other Communist-turned-City-Missionary had discovered the writings of Marx at the age of 20, been arrested at Hyde Park in 1922 and fined £2 for a provocative speech. He later described himself thus: *'though mistaken, I was quite sincere; I was out for revolution and destruction, honestly believing the present system to be past mending.'* In his native Wales and back in London he studied Communist literature, denounced Christianity as a brake on the wheels of progress, and even contemplated a journey to Moscow *'in order to rub shoulders with my "Comrades"of the Third International'*. But a relative had arranged lodgings for him in what turned out to be the home of a City Missionary. *'He was so patient and courteous; argue as I did, he always quietly insisted that the one road to human betterment was by the Cross of Calvary, and that human uplift is the work, not of man, but of God. What men need is a vision of God, a change of heart, a new birth from above.'* The young Communist went on, *'At length, after three days' inward struggle and a drunken bout (the devil's last kick, as they say), I accepted Christ as my Saviour and surrendered myself to His service. This happened after spending eight regrettable years in the anti-Christian war.'*

12
The Great War – and after

Wars change places, and the 'war to end all wars' changed London. Yet the Great War of 1914–18 was, in the main, fought at a distance. There were air raids by Zeppelins and Gotha bombers that claimed the lives of some 700 people, but music halls continued to entertain and couples danced their nights away in the city's halls though they had a dark walk home because lamps were painted navy blue in order not to attract attention from the air. It was as though London held the war at arm's length and continued the business of living.

Shortly after the declaration of war the Government took over a large part of the cattle market at Islington, and temporarily converted it into a transport depot. Within a very short time some 1,500 troops were bivouacked there, and until the depot closed they had the local missionary's interest and attention. The military authorities welcomed him, encouraging him in the work. As was its practice, the LCM was right where the people were with missionaries engaged at barracks in Colchester, Aldershot and on Salisbury Plain, as well as local men meeting local needs in areas such as Islington.

War on the Home Front

The London City Mission was engaged in a war on two fronts, according to its 1915 Annual Report. *'The great European war into which our Empire has been plunged is universally recognised as one of the saddest which has occurred in the whole history of the world. The many millions of combatants engaged in it, the varied and frightful implements of destruction employed, and the terrible carnage resulting, are unprecedented. Nevertheless, the righteousness of our nation in taking part in this awful conflict is acknowledged far and wide by the nations of the earth. It is felt that we are fighting for the cause of liberty, for justice, for the sacredness of international treaties.'* And most Londoners would have said 'Amen' to that. But the

Report went on, '*This earthly conflict, however, terrible as it is, only typifies one which is still greater, one in which every true Christian must take a part; viz.: the conflict between light and darkness, between truth and error, between sin and righteousness; the tremendous spiritual conflict between Christ and the Great Adversary of mankind.*'

While the nation was at war against its enemies in the trenches of France and Belgium, the mission waged war with the powers of darkness in the city of London. Things were not easy. April 1914 had seen 375 missionaries engaged in the work, but a year later there was a reduction of 15, '*due to the Society's decreased receipts of late years from legacies*'. Economies had been made '*by spending less upon Christian literature, by reducing all salaries by ten per cent, by members of the Committee increasing their own subscription by twenty per cent ...*' Manpower was to be further reduced. Not only had two missionaries signed up for active service, but 2,000 young mission-hall men did too. By the end of 1915, that number had risen to 5,000 and many of them never came back.

Because of the carnage of war, the LCM was acutely aware of its responsibility to prepare the servicemen for the possibility of meeting their maker. The Mission saw the spiritual struggle as solemnly urgent. Young men were away from home, many for the first time. Although they were worked hard, they still had time on their hands and many had death on their minds. Walter Prentice, the missionary to coalies, was seconded for a time to minister to the troops. '*I spent a month in one of the rest camps at Folkestone, and as my lodging was right opposite the camp, I could hear the boys as they often came tramping along, sometimes at five o'clock in the morning, a thousand or more strong. The boys who were going out to the Front for the first time were generally whistling. It was not so with the men who were going out for the second, third, or even the fourth time. Often I have been privileged to cheer some of these sad hearts, and some had the soundest reasons for being sad. One man said to me:"I have just been on leave to bury my wife, and am leaving behind five motherless children." Sometimes it was my part to send a wire to wife or mother, or to secure a pass for a woman who had been travelling many miles to have perhaps a last look at her loved one who had not had leave to see her before embarkation. In this one camp alone I distributed 20,000 copies of the Word of God.'*

An appeal went out to the Society's supporters to join in the effort.

THE WAR!

How to Assist The London City Mission During the Present Crisis.

1 – By Daily Prayer that God will enable the Committee to keep every Missionary at the post of duty.

2 – By emergency gifts, of whatever amount, to meet current expenses. The latter average £1,000 weekly.

3 – By grants of Christian Literature for use among the Troops. Booklets would be very acceptable.

4 – By gifts of Surgical Aid Letters and Cast-off Clothing for the deserving and Suffering Poor.

5 – By circulating the Society's Periodicals, this helping to advertise its Daily Work and ever-recurring Needs.

The other side of war

The war was not very old when it became clear that even such a horrific happening could have some good effects. *'Grievous as the present war has already been to our nation, it has not been without its benefits. Whilst, on the one hand, it has desolated many thousands of British homes, robbed the nation to some extent of the flower of its youth, brought serious financial loss to many of the professional and commercial classes, caused many employees to lose their situations, and raised the price of the necessaries of life to a point which is sorely trying to the poor and industrial classes, it has on the other hand, provided work for certain classes, shut the mouths of anti-Christian Socialists, who have been scandalised by the action of their Socialistic brethren in Germany, and done much to bridge over the chasm between the classes and the masses in our own country. Rich and poor have fought side by side, and the bonds of sympathy between them have been greatly strengthened. Best of all, it has solemnised the nation. The spirit of indifference with regard to religious matters, which it has been so difficult for Christian workers to deal with, has to some extent passed away. A ready ear has been given to the message of the Gospel. In some parts it may almost be said that a wave of religious revival has passed over the land. ... They (missionaries) have taken advantage of the opportunity, have visited the bereaved in their homes, and in some cases have won them to Christ.'*

A further two years into the conflict brought another appraisal of the situation. The war, which had been the cause of untold sorrow to so many of every class, had also brought material benefit to a large proportion of the poor. Unemployment was almost at vanishing point and some who had never before worked found employment and were earning from £2 to £3 weekly. Women were much in demand to take the place of men serving in the Forces, and most women showed a spirit of self-sacrifice and revealed strengths that had been hidden in peace time. Now they were actually earning good wages for their long working hours. While the author of the appraisal said that some women wasted much of their hard-earned money, he admitted that a considerable number made good use of what they earned, quite transforming their homes. New furniture was gradually taking the place of the old, and for the first time many who had previously been very poor enjoyed some home comforts.

There were benefits even for the residents of lodging houses. Before the war, a missionary who worked in lodging houses nearly every night met hundreds of men – both young and old – walking the streets looking for food and shelter, most of them ragged and dejected. The war changed all that. Where then there were hundreds, now he could hardly find ten. In one lodging house that accommodated 300 and was regularly completely full, there was now hardly anyone. Where had they gone? About half of them went into the Forces and for the rest there was ample employment. Casual work was available at the docks, wharves and markets. Even older men, who previously were pushed aside, now found jobs and were better off than they had been for years. And not only had competition been lessened, but wages were forced up. *'"The knights of the road" too, are sharing in the general prosperity,'* one missionary noted, when considering his district. *'Four years ago there were 28 Casual Wards accommodating 1,250 tramps. To-day, according to the census taken by the L.C.C. on the night of February 9–10, the inmates numbered only 89.'*

Missionaries, most of whom were total abstainers, noted an interesting fact. It seemed that there was less drunkenness in their districts than formerly, with the result that in the rougher areas there were fewer domestic quarrels and fights. This was attributed to the increased price of alcohol, and to the restricted hours during which it was allowed to be sold. Official statistics appear to support this view, as sales of beer and spirits greatly decreased. A public-house missionary, who thought over the matter carefully, wrote *'On the whole I think there has been a steady decrease in drinking habits amongst men ... But what shall be said about the women? There was a time when respectable women would have scorned the idea of being seen in a public-house, but now in some parts of my district certain houses are absolutely full of women. Young women as well as old ...'*

A helping hand

One missionary commented on the dark side of the war's effect on London. *'The war has been a sad blow to many persons in my district. Aged widows and widowers have had to part with sons who were their main support ... The increased price of food, also, makes it difficult for people with large families.'* Practical in their approach as ever, London City Missionaries sought to help through their Thrift Clubs. *'By this means, during the past year, £12,228 10s 3d has altogether been saved by the poor, which might otherwise have been squandered.'* The missionary who had the largest club reported, *'A considerable increase has taken place in the membership of the Thrift Clubs, owing to the enlargement of the Children's Section.... The membership of the Clubs has increased from 3,281 to 3,721. The amounts paid out in the men's section were, for sickness, £509 10s 10d, for death claims, £255; in the women's section, for sickness, £350 19s 0d, for death claims, £204; in the children's section (in which death only is insured against), £6. This left £3,060 16s 1d to be distributed at Christmas. The result has been that many homes have been made brighter, than would otherwise have been the case, in times of distress caused by sickness and death.'* Another LCM missionary stated that the meetings for his Thrift, Boot and Coal clubs were held once a week in the afternoon, and that he took the opportunity of conducting a Gospel meeting at them. These, he said, *'were greatly appreciated by hard-working women, who bring their children, and in many cases these meetings are the only chance they have of hearing the Gospel.'*

Strangers in a strange land

The Mission was not only at work among Londoners, it has always had a heart for the whole population of the metropolis, regardless of nationality, and there were some strangers who needed to be cared for. During the early stages of the war, Belgian refugees arrived in great numbers in the city's railway stations. For several days in succession train after train drew up, each filled with traumatised men, women and children who had fled from the invaders of their country, all unsure of what their welcome would be in Britain. Many were in a state of utter destitution. A missionary, who was commissioned by Headquarters to meet the incomers, said that all who watched them arriving found it a heart-rending experience. He distributed tracts in Flemish and French, went to the centres where Belgian refugees met, and twice weekly visited the Belgian wounded soldiers in hospitals – often 40 to 50 of them. The contact did not stop there as he had access to Belgian Refugee Hostels where he gave tracts and discussed Scripture, as well as taking Sunday afternoon open-air services in French in Soho, monthly meetings for War Refugees in a YMCA hall and visiting the people in their homes.

Bruised and broken

Others were also arriving from Belgium and France; men horribly wounded who had witnessed things they would never forget. *'Here is an avenue of Christian service that angels might covet,'* wrote one missionary. *'For these men have looked into the face of death ... In the Wandsworth Hospital, for example, where nearly 2,000 wounded are housed, including 400 blind, patients represent nearly every county in the Kingdom, and most of the Overseas Dominions.'* Sadly, when conflicts cease, wounds don't immediately heal and some never do. The end of World War I brought peace between nations but it left victims on both sides of the conflict who never knew peace again. Missionaries going door to door around their districts found themselves cast in the role of counsellors, and untold hours of their time were spent listening to men broken in body and spirit who were trying to piece lives together out of the wreckage and the horror of what they had been through, and the knowledge that although they returned home, 124,000 Londoners did not.

One of those who did not return was a tragic loss to the City Mission. The Buxton family had played a pivotal part in the society since Thomas Buxton became its first Treasurer, and young Captain Andrew Buxton would, no doubt, have continued to serve the Committee as his forebears had done. But it was not to be. He was killed in action in his 38th year. Despite his relative youth, he had already served as a missionary superintendent, and had shown a special interest in the work in Bethnal Green and Canning Town.

Homes fit for heroes

Having come home from the war with the promise ringing in their ears that they would be provided with 'homes fit for heroes', the heroes did not want to live with their in-laws for ever. Dr Christopher Addison's Housing and Town Planning Act (1919), which encouraged the construction of subsidised housing, brought the dream of a 'home of our own' just one step nearer to becoming a reality, even if that home was actually owned by the LCC. The Government's decision to facilitate the provision of local authority housing was not only motivated by a wish to see people comfortably settled after the trauma of war, it also took into account the unpredictable nature of grass-root politics. Marxism and revolutionary thinking were thick in the air, and men who had fought for their country in the trenches might decide to fight for their rights in London. *The money we are going to spend on housing is an insurance against Bolshevism and Revolution,'* the Parliamentary Secretary to the Local Government Board stated. So it was agreed that any costs involved in the building of these homes that exceeded a penny on the rates would be met centrally.

With regard to new building, LCC set itself some high ideals. The standard was to have estates with 12 houses per acre, no flats above three storeys, and most dwellings one or two storey houses in blocks of two to four. Services were to be provided that enabled people to travel into town to work, because the majority of tenants for the new estates moved out from grossly overcrowded districts such as Bermondsey, Southwark and Spitalfields and still worked in those areas. Downham was one such estate. Although the distance was not far – Downham is just seven miles from St. Paul's – it was another world. Instead of alleyways of small flats, most without adequate sanitary arrangements, the estate had 6,071 houses, all with inside bathrooms. The streets were wide for the day, though now they are crowded with cars. When the first residents moved in, personal transport would have been on two wheels rather than four. For longer journeys there was a choice of tram, bus or train – the latter from Downham's own railway station, Grove Park.

The 36,000 original tenants were families. As the houses had between three and five rooms – apart from 216 two-roomed flats – few would be allocated to single people, couples without children, or older people past child-rearing age. Consequently the age profile of the estate at the end of the 1920s was young, and it took two or three generations to change it into the more natural mix it is today.

Downham and similar estates were virtually brand new towns. The London City Mission recognised the opportunities they afforded and placed missionaries in them, provided men and money became available. Almost as soon as Downham was built the LCM was enabled to place Charles Penfold there, in 1927, thanks to a supporter who shared the Mission's vision. '*A gentleman has generously promised to provide a guarantee of £100 per annum for at least three years, so that visitation on City Mission lines may be inaugurated.*' It was not long before Penfold was hard at work, work of an unusually dramatic nature: '*Eager to acquaint himself with his new constituency the Downham missionary took advantage of the phenomenal frost of December 20th last when upwards of 5,000 casualties were reported in the London area. He visited the injured, whose names were published in the local press.*' Soon the LCM had its own premises on the estate. Howard Hall, seating 250 people, was provided by two Cheshire women, Miss Mary Howard and her sister Elizabeth. The report of the hall's opening, makes interesting reading. '*The Estate is good to behold: wide roads planted with trees, refreshing lawns, hundreds of well-kept gardens, and snug-looking villas occupied for the most part by families formerly domiciled in slum areas south of the Thames. The work has made a good beginning. Over 200 children have joined the Sunday School, and the adult meetings promise well.*'

What has been seen on the Downham Estate is only a tiny sample of the work that the LCM was involved in as new districts grew up in Becontree and Dagenham, Morden and St. Helier, and many other parts of London. In addition, it continued much of its older work in the slum areas and workplaces of the capital. The new Howard Hall was added to the list of about 150 halls from which missionaries ministered to their districts.

Throughout the 1920s, many of the War's heroes moved to new homes, and found City Missionaries knocking at their doors.

13

Strikes, Depression and Unemployment

'War lays a burden on the reeling state,
And peace does nothing to relieve the weight.'
William Cowper

'The Unhealthy Areas Committee of the Health Ministry are arranging to make a personal inspection of London's slums. It is estimated that 184,000 persons are living in slum areas where the death-rate is very much higher than in the rest of London.'
The LCM Magazine, 1920

'At the beginning of the 1920s the belief began to circulate, for the first time at a popular level, that there were no longer any absolutes: of time and space, of good and evil, of knowledge, above all of value.'
Paul Johnson, A History of the Modern World, 1983

'A new life is born within (London's) boundaries every three minutes, but of the children born 10,000 die in their first year.'
London Statistics, 1925

'The generosity of London is great. The annual income of its charities is about £14,000,000, most of which is distributed.'
(ibid)
Assessments of the LCM, published in 1924

'In these days of infidelity and indifference what is needed is the simple Gospel, simply told. The LCM exactly meets the need.'
The Rt Hon. Sir W. Joynson Hicks Bart., MP

'The LCM is the best answer to those who tell us that the old-fashioned views about the Bible are out-of-date.'
Sir Thomas Inskip KC, MP

'The Mission is a safeguard for the whole of London. It raises a barrier against the forces of evil and promotes everywhere public order and goodwill.'
W. G. Bradshaw CBE

'I heard that (a man from my district whom I knew well) had been arrested for burglary. I appeared at his trial and spoke for him,...and the Recorder imposed only a light sentence. I visited him in Wandsworth gaol, and had a heart to heart talk. I was at the prison gate on the morning of his release and accompanied him home....'
City Missionary's Annual Report, 1923.

The 'war to end all wars' was over; the heroes were home – albeit many of them mutilated or shell-shocked – and the world was at a new beginning. That may have been what some felt like at the dawn of the 1920s. But the harsh reality was different, inflation shrank the value of a shilling in a woman's purse and the state of industry meant that a man was more likely to queue for a job than to get one. It was the custom of the London City Mission to make an annual appeal in aid of the poor towards the end of the year. This was discontinued during World War I as there seemed to be no need for it. The number of men serving in the Forces meant that there were plenty of jobs at home, and for the first time people who had always been poor were able to afford some of life's little luxuries. But now it all came crashing down, and many of the little luxuries found their way into pawn shops.

Missionaries reported that children in their districts were starving, really starving, and that their helpless mothers were in black despair. And who could blame them? '*A., Army reserve man, wife and three children,*' was the heading in one missionary's report. It went on, '*Served four years in France, was twice gassed, and discharged with allowance of 4s 6d weekly. Had out-of-work pay later. Home a wreck. Most things sold for food. His Mons Star and mother's wedding ring first to go. Furniture followed, even the baby's chair. Starts off each morning at five o'clock in quest of work, returns about ten, hungry and tired out. The children practically starving.*' That report was published in London City Mission's Magazine in 1921, and beside it is a photograph of a missionary in a home in his district. It shows a painfully thin mother with her six undernourished children, one of them with legs like sticks. And the story behind the photograph? '*F., a consumptive, with a weak wife and six children. Their plight was terrible. I secured them a wholesome spread and would have followed the case up, but it was too late. Broken in the fight with disease and poverty F. died. Soon after, his wife, faced with the problem of providing for six children, failed mentally, and was taken to an asylum, and the chidren removed to an Institution.'*

When nothing was left to pawn

At door after door LCM missionaries met desperate scenes of abject poverty. *'D., a widow, tailoress, four children. No work for months. Youngsters half-starved, and shivering with cold. No fire, no food, nothing to pawn. One boy taken to Infirmary a week ago suffering from exhaustion through lack of nourishment, according to the doctor.' 'B., an ex-Service man, wife and eight children. Eldest boy on reaching Army age, joined up. Eldest girl just dismissed from factory through slackness of work. Other children when seen were almost naked. Mother is delicate, nearly dropping for want of nourishment. Husband, a carman, returned from France to find his firm had sold their horses and substituted motors. A decent fellow, willing, able-bodied, but inwardly broken.'* London has always had its poor; but what was new in the early Twenties was that people who had previously thought of themselves as able to cope were also spiralling down into poverty. It was little wonder that the LCM felt the need to make an appeal for funds in aid of the poor; the Mission had to do something to help.

It was not that those who found themselves destitute were doing nothing for themselves. Far from it. Men queued for hours outside docks and factory gates in the hope of getting a day's work (though that means of hiring labour was slated by Lord Shaw in 1920), and employers – who were themselves hard-pressed – sometimes exploited the situation, paying less than they should have done because they knew workers were desperate for whatever they were offered. Unemployed Londoners were known to take possession of public buildings to use as headquarters, food centres or shelters for the homeless. The situation was getting ugly. Not for the first time Britain faced unrest that could have sparked a revolution. And that prospect worried the government because the police had gone on strike for a pay increase in 1918, and the authorities were unsure where officers would stand if there were widespread disruption.

Mass unemployment came about for a combination of reasons: the demobilisation of soldiers who had served in the forces, a post-war industrial slump and fear curtailing investment, among them. The increasing popularity of socialism and the effect of the Russian Revolution, shattered expectations of the good life that was to follow the trauma of war, price rises and food shortages all added fuel to the fire. In 1920, Unemployment Insurance was extended from its original narrow band of industries to cover most industrial workers. But even so, men losing their job still pushed their families below the poverty line.

The hurt hits home

City missionaries sympathetically working among the poor, were not immune to the crisis themselves. A senior member of the Mission's staff presented a paper of 'Facts and Suggestions' to the Committee in September 1920. In it he stated that missionaries were living on or below the poverty line. *'Considering recent increases in rent and travel, with the prospect of still dearer bread and fuel, a married man requires at least £4 weekly. The present average is under £3 – the pre-war value of which is 24/-. At the moment a sovereign is worth about 7/6. The need of the men is desperate ... NOTE: Unless the Society offers a living wage suitable candidates are out of the question, while the best of the present staff will be tempted to resign.'* But candidates did continue to come.

Forty-six were accepted as probationers between 1920 and 1925, 111 between 1925 and 1930. By the time the LCM reached its Centenary in 1935, 2,297 men had served in total.

Christian networking

By the 1920s, LCM's earlier regulation against missionaries giving direct financial help (however commendable its purpose) had been quietly set aside. The Relief Fund, boosted by an annual appeal, provided help that the missionaries could draw on for the people of their district. But there was still much scope for missionaries to put generous Christians in touch with special cases and to find other sources of assistance. Nowadays, what they did would be called networking. One man who visited a family of six in a furnished room, found the parents and four children in a pitiful state. The father had served 21 years in the Army, retiring just after the end of the War with the rank of Sergeant-Major on a pension of 18/- weekly. This he had taken in a lump sum in order to purchase a business. But the economy was in a slump and his business venture failed. When the missionary called, they were living in a room provided for them by the Red Cross and for which they paid 17/6 weekly, taken from the man's unemployment insurance. What could be done for them? The missionary found them an empty room and bought them a second-hand bed and bedding. A member of the aristocracy was prevailed upon to supply blankets and other necessities. Two chairs and a table were begged from elsewhere and the family moved into their new home. But, as the man from the Mission was not merely a social worker, the room was dedicated in prayer and the missionary preached to the family. Their response must have encouraged him. *'Although they "never heard the like," their gratitude was beyond bound. Work was secured for the husband, and from that point recovery was rapid. Father and mother have come to know the Saviour as a result. The children attend Sunday School, and in no home in the district am I a more welcome visitor. I quote the case to show that spiritual good often follows so-called social effort.'* Similar networking went on in the Parish of St. Barnabas, where the missionary acknowledged his gratitude to the *Daily Sketch* Relief Scheme that assisted (by coupons) with food, coals, milk, oatmeal and beef tea. A local restaurant also provided him twice a week with gallons of soup and a bread-and-butter pudding of large dimensions for the aged and very poor children of his district (1928).

Such support, however, could not reach everyone, and many fell deeper into debt and despair. Not all were helped by Unemployment Benefit; some still had to rely on Poor Law provision and, even in the 1920s, tens of thousands of Londoners were in workhouses or their equivalent. Part of the regular work of many missionaries was to visit such places in their districts. The missionary in Lower Holloway said that the one in his area slept 80 men and was always full. As well as visiting the residents there, he held a Sunday Service for them, with between 40 and 50 attending. The residents listened attentively, showed due respect to God's Word, and *'sang heartily if not harmoniously'*.

When the crunch came

Socialism, which had gained support during and after World War I, did not seem able to make a radical change to the problems of the 1920s, and people became disenchanted with left-wing politics. Many Labour councillors, who had won their seats in the years immediately after the War, lasted just one term. Partly this was in response to labour's militant wing. Industrial unrest had resulted in a ground-swell of strikes which came to a head in 1925 when mineowners announced that they were to cut the wages of their workers and the Trade Union Congress indicated its support of the miners. The Conservative Government made funds available to restore the miners' wages to their previous rate. Some months later, the mine owners changed tack, saying that not only were there to be wage cuts, but working hours would increase at the same time. If miners did not accept these conditions, they were told, they would be shut out of the pits. The TUC met on 1st May 1926 and called a General Strike '*in defence of miners' wages and hours*'. It was to start two days later.

Londoners were, of course, not miners. The only way that the mine owners decision would have affected them was by a reduction in the price of coal. But the country was in no mood to think along these lines. Railwaymen, transport workers, dockers, builders, iron and steel workers, and printers were immediately called out by the TUC. Shipyard workers, engineers and others followed later. In response the government struggled to maintain basic services using volunteer staff. Four days later the Chairman of the Royal Commission on the Coal Industry went into discussions with the TUC. A deal was struck on 11th May and the General Strike called off. However, it came unstuck at the miners' end and they remained on strike for a further five months. The following year legislation was passed which made striking in support of another industry and mass picketing illegal. With the mood of the country being as it was, it is quite remarkable that things did not spiral into revolution.

Where was the London City Mission in all of this? In the main, its missionaries were still walking the streets of their districts, still handing out tracts and preaching the gospel, still networking with benefactors to help the poor, and still speaking with working men, even when they were on strike. Missionaries were not politicians; they were not part of the establishment, nor were they managers' men. But they were human and they had their own views on things. One, who worked in Islington, commented, *'I came in contact with ... costermongers, street traders, buyers of rags and old bottles, tinkers, organ grinders, casual labourers, road sweepers, and so on. Quite half the men are of this class, the others being artisans, though irregular employment and the consequent hardship are all too common. "The dole" has a bad effect upon these men, especially the unmarried. The "something for nothing" policy gradually degrades, breeds a dislike for work, and brings temptation in its train. It has increased street gambling, and attendance at billiard saloons, cinemas and public houses.'*

Winter Relief Fund

Despite 'the dole', the LCM recognised that there were still far too many in real need. The Magazine of December 1927 reported that the Mission's Winter Relief Fund was now completely exhausted. An urgent plea was made, so that missionaries could continue to give help in cases of genuine need. Gifts of money, clothing, fruit and toys were especially mentioned. Following the appeal, the editorial goes on to say that the recent Finance Act made it possible for Income Tax to be deducted from contributions to charitable institutions, thus providing an increase of 25 per cent on contributions given under the scheme. The LCM has greatly benefited from Deeds of Covenant since then, and continues to do so today under the successor Gift Aid Scheme. No doubt some of those responding to the 1927 Winter Relief Fund Appeal were among the first to have their Income Tax put to charitable use in this way.

Missionaries who had been with the LCM for years found the 1920s hard, but how much harder must it have been for a young man just starting the work. One such went to his first placement in the slums of Southwark in mid-1925, just when unrest was reaching its peak. Eighteen months later, he wrote an account of his service. Two things make it of special interest. First, there is not a word about industrial unrest because for many in the slums life just went on; and second, because he himself was from the slums. Despite his youth, or perhaps because of it, he had his ups and downs. But at least he had the honesty to share them.

Early impressions

This young man's memory of his first year was one of steady plodding, of getting down to the business of walking the streets. It was hard ministering in the slums even though that was his own background, as he was coming back with his eyes open to what it was really like. Of sin, he says, *'Sometimes its expression is hideous, sickening, unspeakable. What else, humanly speaking, could one expect with so many large families packed into little back rooms?'* Yet even in these poor back rooms a surprise awaited him, and that was what people who hardly had enough to live spent their money on. He found wireless sets and gramophones in their homes, and the people in his area went to the cinema regularly and even had occasional trips in a charabanc. Where they got the money for their entertainments was a mystery to him. Although he found a dismal ignorance of Christian things, those who had had contact with missionaries over the years held the LCM in affection. He tried to build on that.

Having been under the impression that mission work would be easy – though it is hard to imagine where that idea came from – our young man was soon disillusioned. But that did not close his mind. 'One lesson however we learned early: the only way to get hold of people and really interest them in sacred things was to love them. Not easy! Many were and are so unloveable! But it worked. Love in the heart and prayer on the lips opened doors that for long had been closed against the Gospel. It also disposed many to listen who were formerly prejudiced, or sceptical, or disinclined to attend to spiritual things.' He was a busy man, forming, among other things, a choir for the young people and a Bible Class for young men, visiting the sick and aged and holding open-air meetings in various parts of his district. 'At first we were taken for the tallyman, or rent collector, or insurance agent; but the man who preaches Christ in the street, and holds forth in the Hall, will soon be known if not welcomed as he passes from door to door in the parish.' There were conversions during his first 18 months of service, and they must have more than balanced his times of disillusionment.

The work of the London City Mission went on through the unrest of the Twenties. It had braved such times before, and it would meet them again. And when it did the missionaries were still going about their business, walking the streets, knocking the doors, and inviting people to put their trust in Jesus.

14

Jews in Danger

'*There is one nation not confined to any one division of the world, but who are found in them all – the Jews.*'
The LCM Magazine, March 1837

'*At a Hampstead Synagogue the Gospels are read Sabbath by Sabbath, and if these are placed on a plane lower than the Law and the Prophets, the bare fact that they commend themselves to the congregation is surely a sign of the times.*'
J. Newcombe Goad, 1924

'*I had come across anti-semitism in Eastern Europe before, but I thought racial persecution belonged to another age. Half-civilised peoples might still indulge in it but surely not the Germany I had known. It seemed a horrifying nightmare from which I must wake up ... This was not mob violence, such as I had witnessed in the tense days of emotion at the outbreak of war in Paris in 1914 when the crowds, surging along the Grand Boulevards, wrecked several German-owned establishments. This was Government-directed and Government-inspired hate.*' Sir Evelyn Wrench, owner of *The Spectator*, 1940.
Quoted by Michael Burleigh, *The Third Reich*, 2000

'*In Innsbruck, on the night of November 9/10, 1938, SS veterans were ordered to change into civilian clothes, and to await lists of Jews supplied by the local Plenipotentiary for Aryanisation... These men regarded their selection as a "special honour", even if what they did that night made a few of them physically sick. Feil then dispatched these squads to a particular street*

where they were to kill "with as little noise as possible" the named
male members of three Jewish families whom none of the killers knew
personally...'
Michael Burleigh, *The Third Reich*, 2000

'Although persons who ... afflict you may assume the Christian
name, they act quite contrary to the example and precepts of Jesus of
Nazareth.'
Letter to London's Jews, from the Committee of the LCM,
1841

On 4th October 1936, *'over 2,000 blackshirts assembled. Their*
route was blocked in Cable Street by an overturned brick lorry ...
In the "Battle of Cable Street", anti-Fascists fought the police to prevent
them from clearing the barricade. ... Belatedly, the Home Secretary
ordered Mosley to call off the March. This was seen as a decisive
victory by the Jewish People's Council against Fascism and Anti-
Semitism.'
Roy Porter, *London, a Social History*

In the 1930s a new stream of refugees began to arrive in London – Jews fleeing from a Germany ruled by Adolf Hitler. Anti-Semitism has been around for two thousand years. The question is not, does it exist, but where has it currently boiled over? In the 1930s there was no doubt about the answer; it was boiling up in Europe. In the following decade upwards of six million Jewish people lost their lives. While the starkest evidence of the growing evil was to be seen in Germany, anti-Semitism was also an issue in England in the Thirties. London had a resident Jewish community continuously since the days of Oliver Cromwell. The majority were bankers and merchants, traders in gold and precious stones. During the 18th century there was steady growth in the size and wealth of the community, most of whom had their roots in the Sephardi community of Mediterranean Jews.

Other Jews, Ashkenazis from central and eastern Europe, first arrived during the 18th century and were poorer than their Sephardi brothers. They also tended to live close together and so formed the beginning of virtual ghettos. Prior to their coming, anti-Semitic feeling had, in part, been based on jealousy of business acumen and wealth. But the coming of the Ashkenazi people brought a fear of the unknown and a distrust of the ghetto. Dickens' portrayal of Fagin was a typical result.

Although they were allowed to settle in London, Jewish people were discriminated against and did not have full rights as citizens. When Lionel de Rothschild was elected to Parliament, he was unable to take his seat until he had been elected for the fifth time and, even then, only by special resolution. Nor could he, or any of his fellows, graduate from an English or Welsh university, because that involved the taking of a Christian oath. Subtle it may have been in official circles, but anti-Semitism was present nonetheless. It was not so subtle on the streets.

By 1900, the Jewish population in London was over 100,000, and had been increasing dramatically since 1881 with the admission of thousands of escapees from Poland and other parts of Russia in the aftermath of pogroms. Jewish people accommodated the refugees and the communities grew, becoming islands within London, notably in Whitechapel where 'the streets... from Houndsditch to Vallance Road in the east were transformed into a foreign, Yiddish-speaking town' (Stephen Inwood, *A History of London*, p.413ff). Not all Jewish people were isolationist. For example, the Rothschild family built Rothschild Buildings in Flower and Dean Street for the benefit of the poor of their own and the Gentile community. But the strangeness of the growing communities, coupled with their increasing dominance of housing, shops and business-life in parts of the East End, meant that there was an undercurrent of anti-Semitism. There had been incidents of violence before World War I, but the 1930s witnessed more serious rioting, especially in Limehouse and Bermondsey, sparked by the blackshirts of Oswald Mosley's National Union of Fascists.

Into this fraught climate came about 30,000 more Jews, desperate to escape the unspeakable and, so far as many here in Britain were concerned, the unbelievable reality of Nazi Germany. Once World War II began, little more was seen of Mosley but anti-Semitism did not vanish overnight. Throughout the war it was to be found in various guises — Jews were spying for the Gestapo, said some in 1939. Jews were the first to flee London when the bombing started, it was rumoured in 1940. It was Jews who caused the stampede in which hundreds died at Bethnal Green, it was gossiped in 1943. In such a climate, these new arrivals, many of them children separated from parents, found themselves in a strange and frightening land. Among all the other helpers who came to them in their need were missionaries of the LCM, showing no prejudice or discrimination, but eager to help and comfort – and, with sensitivity, to raise the great question of the identity of the true Messiah.

Prepared

Because the LCM had been ministering to the Jewish community ever since the Mission was formed back in 1835, they were aware of the need, and had already established a presence in the predominantly Jewish districts. While the missionaries were first and foremost bearers of the Christian message, they met these displaced people with plain human kindness. In 1939 Bernard Segal, one of two specifically allocated to Jewish people, wrote, '*It needs much sympathy, tact and patience to be a Jewish missionary to-day; and our endeavour is always to show the Jews Christian kindness in order that they may see and know that whatever treatment they receive in other countries, the great heart of Christian England goes out in loving sympathy to the Jewish race. When we consider the German refugee problem ... and as I have personally seen it in all its bitter and cruel persecution, we come to realise that we are face to face with a tragedy almost without parallel. Contact with the sufferers themselves draws one out in desire to render any help within our power to those in such dire distress.*'

That missionary seems to have had access to many Jewish homes in which he enjoyed relationships built over many years. But sometimes he met with a less favourable reception from newcomers. He understood where they were coming from. '*Some ... I have found full of suspicion, in view of the bitter treatment meted out to Jews and non-Aryans in Germany. It is not surprising that some should question our good intentions. But I have told them that true followers of Christ have no hatred against anyone, much less against the people from whom, according to the flesh, came the Saviour of all men.'*

The LCM was not only engaged in speaking to the refugees, it also cared for their bodies. In 1926 it had taken over the Jewish Mission Dispensary in Montague Street, Whitechapel, from an independent committee that had previously administered its affairs. Most of the patients were women and children, although a fair number of men also went for treatment. This was before the days of the National Health Service, and the dispensary was much used by the poor from the Jewish community. Some might argue that this was an underhand way of reaching these people with the gospel, but the missionaries saw themselves doing exactly what their Saviour had done before them, helping people with their problems and, while their hearts were open, telling them the good news that Jesus was the Messiah. As one man put it, *'The need and importance of medical work among Jews from the standpoint of evangelism cannot be exaggerated. I deem it not only human but Christ-like.'*

Jesus the Messiah

When considering mission work among Jewish people it has to be remembered that the Christian does not see faith in Jesus as contrary to Jewish belief, but rather as a fulfilment of true Jewish theology. They look for a Messiah; Jesus is the Messiah. To tell of Jesus is to point these people to the person for whom they are looking and waiting. Consequently, it had been entirely natural for the London City Mission to reach out to the Jewish community from its earliest days, although it did not seem natural to the people to whom they went. Just a year after the Mission's foundation, in 1836, the missionary appointed to work with Jewish people had reported, *'I get very little access at present, and seldom get a second hearing. When I do, and attempt to read, they turn their backs upon me. If I venture to make any remarks, they go away... Still one thing is encouraging, the books in the library for the use of the Jews are read and returned.'*

In 1841 the LCM undertook Jewish evangelism in a serious and systematic way. They wrote a letter, 'To the Children of Abraham, Isaac and Jacob' and delivered, as nearly as they could, a copy to every Jewish family in the metropolis, rich and poor (There were around 30,000 Jews in London at the time):

'Peace be unto you!

We feel it to be very difficult to address you, knowing that an epistle coming to you from Christians will not meet with a cordial reception. We are aware of the causes of your strong prejudice against Christianity, and trust that a candid examination of a few of them may tend, by the blessing of God, to soften that prejudice.

The first we shall allude to is, the bitter persecution your forefathers have endured from ungodly people who called themselves Christians; to which we may add, the oppression and injustice you are exposed to in many countries at the present time. But, although persons who thus afflict you may assume the Christian name, they act quite contrary to the example and precepts of Jesus of Nazareth. So far is He from countenancing cruelty and opposition, that He has said, "Love your enemies, bless them that curse you, do good to them that hate you, and pray for them which despitefully use you and persecute you." This is the spirit He has commanded His disciples to show forth; and He gave us a glorious example of it in His own conduct, and He died on the cross as our ransom and the atonement for sin, being "cut off out of the land of the living for the transgression of His people." Instead of calling down vengeance on His murderers, He prayed, "Father, forgive them; for they know not what they do."

Another cause of your prejudice against Christianity, is the ungodliness you see practised by many of those who call themselves Christians, and whom you consider to be such. But these, we again repeat, are not the followers of Christ. He has commanded His people to be pure and holy, to shun even the thought of wickedness. It is as unfair to charge the sins of such ungodly men on the religion of Jesus, as it would be to charge the evil deeds of Jews on the holy precepts delivered to you by Moses.

The next cause to which we shall allude is, your ignorance of what Christianity really is; and for this ignorance we Christians have in a great measure to reproach ourselves. We have to acknowledge, with shame, that we have not, as a body, shown forth to your people, by our life and conversation, what the Lord has done for your souls, which was our bounden duty; for one of your own brethren, the Apostle Paul, when addressing Gentile believers, says, that salvation has come unto the Gentiles to provoke you to jealousy.

We desire now to set before you what we, as Christians, really believe; and you will see how we are constrained, by the love of Jesus, to intreat you to think seriously of the condition in which you are at present ...'

The letter, a masterpiece of craftsmanship and an example of Christian humility, goes on to outline the basic tenets of Christianity: the acceptance of the Bible as the Word of God; the fact of sin and our responsibility for it; the promise of the Messiah and the coming of Christ in fulfilment of that promise, and God's full and free offer of salvation. Point by point the Committee showed from the Jewish Scriptures where Christians were coming from, and what they believed. The letter ended with a challenge. 'May *our blessed Lord speedily fulfil to you the promise made in the Book of Zechariah* (with which readers would be very familiar): *"I will pour upon the house of David, and upon the inhabitants of Jerusalem, the spirit of grace and of supplications; and they shall look upon me whom they have pierced." O give not all your thoughts to the welfare of your perishing bodies: remember you have never-dying souls, which must be happy or miserable for ever. "Turn ye, turn ye, for why will you die, O house of Israel?"*

It was signed by the Secretaries on behalf of the Committee.

Understood and misunderstood

Such a letter could not but provoke a response, and when it came it was two-fold. Some wrote in high dudgeon at the effrontery of the LCM in writing in these terms. Others, recognising the spirit in which the letter was written, wrote thanking the Committee for the expression of affection and sympathy for the scattered children of Abraham, and encouraging the Mission to persevere in the work in the same spirit. And that is what the LCM has endeavoured to do ever since.

In 1866, a quarter of a century after that letter was written, four missionaries were engaged in Jewish mission work, all of them Jewish Christians. One of them had, at the centre of his district, the Wentworth Street Ragged School, some of whose pupils were from Jewish homes, though he pointed out that they had nothing of Judaism but the name. These youngsters had no education but what they received in the Ragged School, and no other means of learning about Jesus. But although it seems that many parents were happy to accept the education offered (there was then no state schooling) others from the community showed their disapproval by throwing stones through the windows, so necessitating the erection of wire mesh and shutters. And the hard-liners, who had not long before formed themselves into a synagogue, noted those children who attended the school and refused their families relief in times of need. The building in Wentworth Street was very much a community school, a long time before the term had been coined. There were about 1,000 itinerant Jewish glaziers living in the area, originating from Russia, Poland, Turkey and Germany. Most lived in 'hole-in-the-corner lodging houses' and many were happy to accept an invitation to a meal in the relative comfort of the school building. The missionary then started an English class for them, using the New Testament as the means of teaching. The building could only hold 150, and it was usually full.

There can be few harder mission-fields than the Jewish community, partly because of the way they have been treated throughout history by those who called themselves Christians. But people have come to faith in Jesus in ones and twos, though it often resulted in persecution. In March 1889, the LCM's Magazine gave an account of such a conversion and what resulted from it. It must have shown missionaries just what a huge step it was for a Jewish person to make public profession of faith in Christ. *'A Jew, a tailor, who worked at a West End shop, came to me for instruction in the truths of the Christian religion, which I gave him gladly. He then attended my meetings. When this became known, the other Jews employed there charged him with being an apostate. When I was ill in hospital he came to visit me, bringing another Jew with him. We talked about Christ, His love, etc. He then told me that he and his family would soon be baptised. This was reported at the shop among forty of his countrymen. They made all sorts of allegations* against him, laid hands on him, and this drove him away. Still his faith did not waver. He and his six children were baptized ... He obtained work again at another shop; but so soon as it was known there the foreman, being a Jew, brought complaints against him ... and the manager discharged him... Now he works at home, but is hardly able to earn the necessaries of life...' Missionaries to Jewish people have to live with the knowledge that conversion, while it may secure heavenly joy, will almost certainly bring with it trouble on earth. Consequently, this work has to be carried out with great sensitivity.

The Bible in Yiddish

In 1900, a great Zionist Congress was held in London, and an offer of a Bible in Yiddish was made by the Mission to those who attended. Over 100 applications were received and the Bibles were dispatched. An LCM missionary, Marcus Bergmann, had done the translation, believing that the way to a Jewish person's heart was through the language with which he was most familiar. Enquirers and missionaries welcomed the initial print-run of 10,000, and the translation met with an encouraging response. The following letter, literally transcribed, was only one of a number that arrived soon after publication:

'Dear Sir, I have shown the Bible to a friend of mine (who is a Sofar [i.e. a scribe of the Law of Moses]) that he should tell me whether the Bible is correct transilatad. Her was astonished, and wondering how this could be transiletad so corectly, and so word by word, which he has never seen that before. He asked who are you? I told him that you are a missionary preaching the Gospel of Christ. When he heard that, he was still more wondering, put the hand in his pocket, took out 2s 6d, give it to me, which you will find enclosed, that I should get a Bible for him, but it must be such as mine. He should

175

feel very happy, he said, if he could speak to you, as he has a few very important questions to ask you out of the Talmud and the Bible ...'

One missionary received a complaint from a Jewish gentleman to whom he had given a copy, but it was not one that worried him. The man wrote, *'I had done him a great injury by giving him the Bible, because though he comes home late every night from his work, he must read the Bible till the small hours of the morning.'* Bergmann had put hundreds of hours into his work of translation, and God blessed him with the knowledge that Jews became Christians through reading the Yiddish Bible, letters even coming from across the Atlantic to tell him of such conversions.

So, having had a heart for Jewish people, and having been engaged in evangelism among them from 1835, the LCM was well placed to reach out to those who were hurting when, a hundred years later, persecution sent tens of thousands to London. And in the years since World War II the work has continued, in close co-operation with other evangelical missions. The results have not been enormous, but neither have they been negligible.

15

Blitzkrieg!

'The Committee ... discussed measures for safeguarding the staff if war should break out. After adjourning to inspect the basement accommodation, it was agreed to construct a bomb-proof shelter. The Secretary was firm in his contention that the work of the Office should be carried on as usual at the Mission House, feeling that as our Missionaries are in London there was no alternative.'
Minutes of the LCM Committee, 28th August 1939

In the autumn of 1940, over 175,000 people were sheltering in Underground stations each night.

'It was reported that Ridley Hall, Forest Gate, had been seriously damaged by bombs. Other halls that had sustained slight damage were: Downham, Kingston, Morden, Greenwich. Also the dwelling-house at Elkington Road, Plaistow, had received damage to the roof. Two missionaries had lost their homes through enemy action... Missionary Pirie had been slightly wounded in the head. The most serious casualty was J. D. Bowden-Pickstock, who was in his house when it was struck by a bomb, and was now in hospital in a critical state.
A grant of £5 was made to missionary J. A. Payne, whose bicycle was stolen while he was engaged in mission duties.'
Minutes of the LCM Committee, 18th November 1940

'In order to economise in the use of paper, this will be the last issue of the Magazine with the present cover.'
The LCM Magazine, May/June 1942

'*Friends having lavender in their gardens are again reminded of our need for lavender, and for squares of material to make up into little bags. There is great scope for the ministry of the lavender bag just now among the civilian injured in London's hospitals.*'
The LCM Magazine, Sept./Oct. 1944

'*There can be no doubt that there is a wide and deep gulf between the Church and the people... The war... with its general mix-up of the population, has afforded an unequalled opportunity of gaining some general appreciation of the situation.... The evidence of chaplains and others in close touch with all three Services, and with munition factories, may be accepted as conclusive. They testify with one voice to the fact of the wholesale drift from organised religion. The present irrelevance of the Church in the life and thought of the community in general is apparent from two symptoms which admit of no dispute. They are (1) the widespread decline in church going; and (2) the collapse of Christian moral standards.*'
'Towards the Conversion of England', Church of England Report, 1945

'*The Candidates Committee which had met for the first time since April 1939 recommended the following candidates to the Committee for service in the Mission: Frank Hewlett, William Gray and Basil Cole. They were called in separately and questioned. As they answered satisfactorily it was agreed that they should be sent to the Doctor and Examiners...*'
Minutes of the LCM Committee, 12th November 1945

At 11.15 on the morning of 3rd September 1939, 15 minutes after the deadline for Germany to stop all aggressive action against Poland and begin to withdraw from Polish territory, the Prime Minister, Neville Chamberlain, told the people of the United Kingdom, '*No such undertaking has been received and consequently this country is at war with Germany.*' Almost immediately, air-raid sirens wailed over London, and people ran for the shelters fearing that an aerial bombardment was about to devastate the city. It was a false alarm. Most people heard the news of the outbreak of war as they huddled around their wireless sets; but it was not really news at all. By that time it would have been more newsworthy to announce that war had been averted.

Two days previously, Londoners had begun to take farewell of their children as they watched them leave for the relative safety of the countryside. Almost half of the school children, about 395,000 in all, were herded on to trains and coaches, each child labelled and clutching a gas mask. Along with them went 50,000 teachers and a quarter of a million mothers with small children. As the government was expecting the capital to be under prolonged and appalling attack, the evacuation was well planned. The children's parents were not the only ones to miss them. The majority of evacuees were taken from those areas in which the Mission was most active: East and West Ham, Tottenham, Ilford, Leyton, Willesden, Stepney, Poplar and Bermondsey, and on that terrible first Sunday of September, Mission Halls' Sunday School attendance was reduced almost to vanishing point. Within the space of a few hours the homes, streets and halls were cleared of children. The following month LCM's Magazine had a word for those of its supporters who had evacuees billeted with them. '*For years, maybe, you have followed with prayerful interest our work among these* children. *Now they have been removed from our care, and the responsibility for their physical welfare has been transferred from their parents into your sympathetic hands. We believe that you will gratefully avail yourself of the opportunity ... of continuing to exert upon these young lives those Christian influences which we have endeavoured to bring to bear ...'* The first effect of the war on London City Mission was the virtual cessation of its children's work.

Business as usual

Other things did not stop, and that was official. The same magazine, the first since the beginning of hostilities, made that quite clear. The Mission had a century of service behind it. It had worked through social upheaval, the Crimean War, the Boer War and the Great War; there was no way in which the newly declared war was going to interrupt its ministry. Taking Nehemiah as an example, the Mission asked, as he had, 'Why should the work cease?' Then with a great affirmation of faith it moved on, the words of Paul ringing in missionaries' ears. *'I am persuaded that neither death, nor life, nor angels, nor principalities, nor powers, nor things present, nor things to come, nor height, nor depth, nor any other creature, shall be able to separate us from the love of God, which is in Christ Jesus our Lord'* (Rom. 8:38–39).

Suitable Mission Halls were immediately put into use as air-raid shelters. The missionary at King's Cross cleared out the cellars and made room for 75 people to shelter. How it saddened him when the sirens went and the people he had come to love stumbled along darkened streets to the cold comfort of an underground concrete floor. The tea he provided seemed such a little thing. It was not long, however, before some basements were filled with an altogether happier crowd. Within weeks, and quite against the advice of the authorities, child evacuees started to return to London. A combination of predicted air raids not actually happening, homesickness and the strangeness of 'all that countryside', reunited many families once again. By January 1940, over 30 per cent of evacuated children and 90 per cent of mothers with small children were back in the capital. But schools were closed and 50,000 teachers had left the city. Consequently children ran wild in the streets, delighted to be back with their friends and in familiar surroundings. Grasping the opportunity of helping, missionaries began to open their basements as playrooms for returned evacuees. Some even made an effort at running a school. In one hall a visitor found *'fifty girls from eight to fourteen ... busily engaged in arithmetic, under the tuition of the missionary and his wife.'*

When, by the beginning of 1940, not much seemed to be happening, there was relief mixed with a sense of anticlimax. The previous summer LCM missionaries had trained as air raid wardens; others joined the Police Reserve and the Fire Service, and still others the Red Cross. Records note that in January several missionaries returned to full-time service, leaving 72 out of the total of 265 still engaged in the war effort. Most of these were able to maintain their Mission Hall meetings although times had to be arranged to fit their new work patterns. Of course, the missionaries, being the men they were, made use of their work as wardens to tell the gospel.

Bombed!

It was six months later, in July, after France had fallen to the Germans, that the Battle of Britain began with great aerial conflicts over Kent and Sussex. On 24th August, the battle touched London, albeit accidentally. The bombs and incendiary devices were intended for industrial sites south of the city, but German pilots lost their bearings and dropped them on the

East End instead. The following night a retaliatory raid on Berlin was launched, and Hitler responded, 11 days later, with 320 bombers and over 600 fighters. They flew up the Thames Estuary in daylight and discharged their deadly cargoes on industrial targets, the docks and the East End slums. Another raid later that same night was guided by the fires that already raged. This time they aimed for the City, Kensington and Westminster, with devastating effect. Over 400 Londoners were dead by morning, and 1,600 badly injured. The war had reached the heart of London, a year and a day after the outbreak of hostilities. The Blitz was to continue just about every night until the middle of May, 1941.

When the Blitz began, missionaries were immediately in the front-line. Even before reports reached the public through the press, the LCM was only too aware of the widespread distress that Hitler's Luftwaffe had caused in the poorest parts of London. No time was lost. The Mission's War Relief Fund was used to help those in most immediate need. Many Mission Hall people lost everything. One couple salvaged only the two eiderdowns they had been sitting on when their home crashed down about them. Their missionary was able to obtain clothing and other immediate needs. Another family lost not only their home but the breadwinner in the raids. All they managed to salvage was the lid of a piano keyboard, a scullery table and a basket of torn clothes. LCM was not slow to award them a grant. Because many missionaries lived in the heavily-bombed areas, they too sustained loss. A special fund was set up to help them. No missionaries were killed, though one was seriously injured when a bomb struck his house.

'On the night of December 29th, 1940, a dastardly attempt was made by the Nazis to destroy the City of London by fire,' says the March 1941 Magazine. 'The plot failed; but serious loss was sustained by business houses whose premises were destroyed, by the destruction of famous City churches, by disaster to such historic buildings as the Guildhall. The London City Mission was called upon to bear a heavy share of that night's tragedy. Its headquarters at 3 Bridewell Place, occupied for the past sixty-seven years ... was so seriously damaged as to be no longer useable.' The old building was never used again. The society relocated and continued business almost as usual; its work, after all, was to save people not buildings. What did a demolished building matter compared with the family one missionary visited at the time? When he called he discovered a distraught mother whose four-year-old son had been horribly burned when a blazing plane fell out of the air and crashed near him. The following night the woman's brother and his entire family were killed in a raid. Providing her with comfort and support, rather than mourning the destruction of Headquarters, was what the LCM was all about.

So great was the devastation that, by the middle of 1941, one out of every six Londoners had been homeless for a time. No plans were in place to deal with this; people were expected to make their own arrangements. But as the most badly bombed areas were also the poorest, and as many extended families lived in them, often people just had nowhere to go. Government money patched up over a million homes to make them habitable, and it also provided emergency accommodation, often in air-raid shelters and sometimes with the help of LCM missionaries. 'I offered myself as a shelter marshal,' one said, 'realising the great opportunities that would present themselves ... The shelter to which I was attached was a reinforced ground-floor flat, consisting of four rooms, and what was originally intended to be a kitchenette. At the beginning of the raids, bunks had not been provided, and each family brought their own bedding, and laid it on the floor. The scene has to be imagined when I mention that

I have had as many as ninety persons in the shelter at a time ... I decided to try to run a small canteen ... For six months, every night without fail, the shelterers were able to have something for supper before settling down to sleep. ... Meanwhile the spiritual needs of the people were not being neglected. On several occasions I had prayer in the rooms ... many conversations were held.'

God of a crisis?

Much has been made of the resilience of Londoners at the time of the Blitz, and this is borne out by what missionaries reported. Stories abound of families welcoming strangers into their homes, of people giving some of the little they had to those who had nothing at all, and of others struggling to cope in desperate circumstances and still having an amusing quip for the missionary. Some say that there was a greater awareness of the need of divine help, though this is not borne out by statistics. *'Mass Observation looked for signs of a spiritual revival, but could find nothing but a continuing decline in religious observance ... Instead, Londoners did what they had done for the past thirty years, they went to the pictures'* (Stephen Inwood, *A History of London*). LCM's 1944 Annual Report confirmed this. *'It is evident that the drift away from the Churches has assumed alarming proportions. Whereas a few years ago the average of church attendance throughout districts occupied by the Mission was about five per cent, there are now many such districts in which it is doubtful whether more than one person in every hundred has a church attachment of any sort.'*

Having been ferociously attacked for a year from mid-1940, those who lived in the metropolis enjoyed a time of relative peace until the beginning of 1944. Evacuees were back in the city, even those who had left for a second time during the Blitz, and life achieved some kind of normality apart from occasional raids. Missionaries made the most of what opportunities came their way. For example, some combined ARP duties with distributing tracts, others spoke of the Lord to those who answered the door as they collected War Savings contributions, and several incorporated fire duty with visiting in lodging houses and other needy places. As the Magazine said, '*This is the pioneering spirit which has characterised the work of London City Missionaries from the beginning.*' But the LCM's men were not only active on the home front – 18 served in the Forces overseas.

V is for vengeance

Just when it seemed that the war might be nearing its end, things took a turn for the worse as far as London was concerned. Six days after the Allies landed in France, in June 1944, Germany's latest weapons took to the air. The V1 flying bombs had begun (V stood for Vengeance, and that was what it felt like to be on the receiving end) and soon V2 rockets followed. Both were lethal. They carried one ton warheads, the V1s at 470 mph, the V2s at 3,600 mph. Fighter aircraft and ground-based guns shot down about 40 per cent of the V1s, but the rest, and all the V2s, hit home. Unlike the Blitz, when most raids came at night, many of the flying bombs and rockets fell in daytime. The flying bombs coughed their way through the skies like dying motor cars – hence their nickname Doodlebug – then when they ran out of fuel everything went quiet in the air and quieter still on the ground as people searched the sky to see where they would land and in which direction they should run. Doodlebugs killed 1,600 Londoners in two weeks, and badly injured 4,500 others. In the month of July, over 20,000 houses were damaged each day. The war became a war of nerves. '*Perhaps it is not so bad as the Big Blitz, though it is nerve-*

*racking to have it all day. But then the nights were wild with gunfire,
and the great bombs came tearing and whistling down the sky, driving
deep into the earth. These beastly things are only unpleasant if they
explode near you. In the distance they don't sound much'* (Vere
Hodgson in Stephen Inwood, *A History of London*).

While the LCM existed to care for the people of London,
it also had a duty of care to its own staff. Some men had worked
ceaselessly, feeling that the people in their districts needed all
of their time and energy. But that could only go on for so
long, and the strain was beginning to show. In September 1944,
the following short snippet appeared in the society's Magazine.
*'The invasion of the Continent has both begun and become established:
our hearts are buoyed up with the hope of early victory. But with
success there has also come a new trial, the brunt of which is being
borne in London. We cannot now tell the whole story of the flying
bombs, but we may disclose that Mission property has sustained heavy
damage, and that several of our missionaries have suffered the loss of
their homes, although, thank God, life has been spared. But the strain
has been, and continues to be, severe. We have felt it right to encourage
our missionaries and their wives to get away for holidays, wherever
they could make the necessary arrangements. We acted in faith, feeling
sure that the cost would be met; and now we turn to you again, who
have helped us so generously in the past.'*

Forward planning

In the thick of the flying bombs, the LCM was working on an
assessment of post war responsibilities and opportunities. It
had started the war with a staff of 270 missionaries, and
expected to finish it with around 200 as no recruiting had been
done for five years and there were the usual losses through
death, retirement and resignation. Amazingly, supporters had
been generous to a fault over the time of hostilities, and the

Mission had been able to gather a small reserve, but not nearly enough to restore staff to its 1939 level, and the same, if not more, work waited to be done. There was also the issue of Mission Halls, at least 50 of which had been hit in the bombing. Repair and replacement of these premises was seen as a priority. The old Headquarters were replaced by a rented building in Eccleston Street, Victoria. At the time of the assessment, this had been requisitioned by the War Office and was being used by the Salvation Army. Bearing all these practicalities in mind, the assessment concluded, '*As a Mission we are persuaded that the years ahead will make our work increasingly necessary: that it will be more and more the task of Christian men and women to go after the lost, seeing them in their own homes, at their work, amid their pleasures, and confronting them there with the claims of God in Christ. To this we pledge ourselves for the post war years.*'

While the London City Mission was considering the future, V-weapons continued to fall. In the last winter of the war, over 1,000 were aimed in the direction of the city, some to devastating effect. In November 1944, 168 people lost their lives when a Woolworth store at New Cross was hit. On 8th March 1945, in almost the last raid of the war, 134 were killed in Stepney. Then, at 7.40pm on 7th May, the people of Britain heard that the next day was VE day. Victory in Europe had been secured. At 3pm on the 8th, the Prime Minister announced that, '*the German war is at an end*'. Nine hours later, at the stroke of midnight, hostilities ceased. On the following afternoon, Winston Churchill appeared on a balcony above Whitehall to tell the waiting crowd, '*This is your victory, God bless you all!*' London partied. Searchlights played on the night sky, and fireworks danced in between them. Bells rang from every corner of the city where bell-towers still stood, and people sang and danced with friends and strangers.

The May/June 1945 issue of LCM's Magazine carried an article entitled, 'Out of Uniform again – my return to missionary work.' And that was how the Mission saw the peace; it was time to get those plans for post war London down, dusted and into action.

16

Rebuilding

(In 1945) *'With every resource put into the war effort, Britain was effectively bankrupt.'*
Eric J. Grove, *Vanguard to Trident*

'1946 — *Year of Opportunity. War has succeeded in a dozen ways in preventing the spread of the Good News. But now we are at peace again. Let us set forward the Cause of Christ, therefore, with all our hearts.'*
The LCM Magazine, Jan. 1946

Some Results of the Work during the year 1954–55

Missionaries employed	156
Visits and calls	887,842
Visits to Transport workers	78,842
.. Factories, Markets and Docks	17,256
.. Gas Workers	11,704
.. Coalies, costers, Municipal Employees and Newsvendors	12,234
.. Firemen, Police and Postmen	11,397
.. Theatres	8,794
.. Public Houses and Coffee Shops	5,325
.. Welsh, Jews & Foreigners	7,448
.. Lodging Houses	3,802
.. Hospitals & Institutions	14,876
Professed decisions	964
New Communicants and Restored	403
Tracts given	834,159

Prisoners visited	73
Situations found for the unemployed	81
Mission services	27,818
Adults who attended	493,410
Children who attended	533,771
Open-air services	1,600
Mission Hall workers (volunteers)	1,153
Sunday School teachers	968
Sunday School scholars	10,498
Women's Meeting attendants	2,806
Men's Meeting attendants	332

'The late 1940s and 1950s witnessed the greatest church growth that Britain had experienced since the mid-nineteenth century. Historians and sociologists have never come to terms with the growth of institutional religion in Britain between 1945 and 1958.'
Callum G. Brown, *The Death of Christian Britain*, 2001

World War II had ended; there was work to be done. Bomb-sites peppered the city, and the East End was devastated. Much patching and covering of cracks had, of necessity, taken place over the war years – people needed a roof over their heads, even if it was covered with a tarpaulin to keep out the rain. Rationing did not end with the hostilities, nor did food shortages and the chronic shortage of money. Demolishing and rebuilding was a slow affair; and nothing would ever be quite the same again. Unlike after World War I, there was no great drive to build houses, no generous government funding to pay for them. London City Mission was not in the business of town planning, but it did know how to help people rebuild their lives. There was something in the day-to-day ordinariness of the local missionary that reassured people, and something in the challenge of the gospel that told them – if they had a mind to listen – that there could be a new beginning in Jesus Christ. That was the message that LCM missionaries such as Stanley Wilcock took round the doors.

He lived, with his wife and two children, right at the edge of the Downham estate, which can again be taken as a small sample of the LCM's work. In addition to the missionary working the district around Howard Hall, the Mission had placed a second missionary in a different part of the large estate. Stanley Wilcock's patch was what was called an 'open district' because it contained no Mission Hall. His remit was to visit the homes of his district in a systematic way, encouraging any who showed an interest in the faith to attend a local church. The London City Mission is not a church and has never set out to be one. Even where there is a Mission Hall (since 1990 they have been called Christian Centres) in which services are held, people are not 'in membership' and they are encouraged to attend and become members of a local church. The Mission aims to reach the un-churched, to challenge them with the gospel then ease them into congregations where they will be built up in the faith and serve as members of a fellowship. In practice, there have always been a few exceptional halls that are churches in all but name, though none administer the sacraments.

As missionaries go from door to door they meet many needy situations. Stanley Wilcock must have been a welcome visitor in times of difficulty, particularly as he did not discriminate against those whose beliefs differed from his. '*Visitation from house to house is not all giving tracts and preaching door-step sermons. There are practical ways in which we may win the confidence of the people, for we are able to help them from our Relief Fund – help for the woman whose electric meter was robbed while she was out visiting her sick husband in hospital, and the bundle of clothes given to an unemployed Communist with a wife and seven children in sore need of help.*'

A missionary through and through

A gifted photographer, Stanley Wilcock became well known in the area for his slide shows, at each of which he presented the gospel in a simple way. Like many LCM missionaries, the gospel came out of the pores of the man. When he was in a sanatorium recovering from tuberculosis he shared a room with two other men. One evening, hearing them talking too late for her liking, a nurse called to the men to be quiet. They were. But what she neither saw nor heard was that the missionary was kneeling at the bedside of one of his fellow patients, quietly praying with the man who was committing his life to the Lord. The other patient – neither recovered from his illness – also came to know Jesus that night. The men from the Mission were not 'professional Christians' paid to work a 40 hour week then forget about it. First and foremost they were in love with the Lord, and with their servant-hearts they spent themselves sacrificially in the service of the Saviour and the people of London.

The lack of a Mission Hall did not limit the relationships a missionary could build with people in his district. Stanley Wilcock obviously knew Dick well. *'I was visiting Dick's wife, who was dying of cancer. She had been given three months to live. I read to her from the Scripture ... we had a little prayer, and I asked her to put her trust in the Saviour. When I came away with her husband, I felt that this was a golden opportunity. I said to him: "You know, God has been speaking to you very much lately. He has been speaking to you through your dying wife. He spoke to you last November when you came out of prison for that theft, when you lost your job, and the missionary prayed that you might get a job, and you did. He spoke to you one day in September when you were visiting your wife and family in the hop fields, and the missionary ... preached the Gospel beside your bin ... God spoke to you when you lay on your back in ... hospital and you sent for the missionary ... and he spoke to you, Dick, in Alf's parlour on the night of the argument ... Don't let him speak to you once too often.'* Stanley Wilcock's ministry was no hit-or-miss affair. While he did not have a Mission Hall, he had many open doors, doors opened by the fact that the people of Downham knew what they meant to him.

Billy Graham

Downham has always had a higher than average number of young people because of the size of the estate's houses. The missionary would be a familiar sight to them, with his leather bag under his arm, as he passed them playing on the streets, because he was always out and about. From 10am till lunchtime he visited then, after a meal and a rest, he was on the road again, faithfully trudging the streets. It took discipline to engage in that kind of ministry. The missionary at Howard Hall used his premises to provide activities for children and youngsters, keeping their interest with various clubs and meetings. Stanley Wilcock could not do that, but he took bus-loads of the young and the not-so-young to Harringay Stadium, to the biggest Christian meetings London had ever hosted. In 1954 Billy Graham went to the city to hold a six-week-long evangelistic 'Crusade' (as it was termed in the unfortunate jargon of the time). Many of these youngsters were converted there. Long after Billy Graham returned to America the missionary's joy was to show slides of these young converts and to tell an audience what they were going on to do for the Lord.

Events like Harringay may give the impression that people come to faith in an instant, nothing having gone before. But in at least one case, Stanley Wilcock had put in ten years' work before seeing results at a Billy Graham meeting. '*Bill ... came after much persuasion to Harringay last year and was indifferent right up to the moment of the appeal – then, he suddenly went out for Christ. But behind that transaction were prayer, visitation, tracts and contacts. There were seed sowing, preparing and planning, and the period during which Bill seemed to keep the door in his life closed to God and His servants was ten years ... So although the work is urgent in one sense, in another sense I am learning not to worry too much about time – about the time it takes some souls to turn to Christ: the important thing is for me to be doing my job in God's "now".*' It was during the Billy Graham campaign that Harry Vallance, aged 16, got to know the Downham missionary and so came into touch with the LCM. It was to be no passing relationship. A year later Harry became a Christian, and eventually a City Missionary.

Changes good and bad

In the 1960s, some 25 years after going to Downham, Stanley Wilcock wrote of the changes he had seen happening around him. More or less the same changes occurred in all the LCC estates that had been built in the 1920s. *'The terrain ... remains the same, apart from bombed houses rebuilt and four new old people's flatlets raised on spare ground ... Trams went in 1949 ... betting shops have come to both ends of my district and these are not helpful aids to moral advancement. One thing I miss: the groups of delightful flowering shrubs that adorned our street corners ... now we have grass plots ... Today we have ... both parents at work until late afternoon or evening. To the missionary this means many unopened doors, but the proportion could be larger if one did not study people's habits and visit accordingly. Which leads to the subject of affluence. Here, changes are astonishing — television, telephones, and cars: most of them parked in narrow roads. Prosperity has made people affable, but indifferent to religion.'*

Many years later, after serving as both a church-based and work place missionary, Harry Vallance, who was born and brought up in Downham, was asked to take over Howard Hall in 1990. The main thing that struck him on his return was the traffic. As a lad kicking a ball about on the streets with his friends, a passing cyclist was an irritation! Having been away for 28 years, he noticed one other striking improvement on the estate. The Downham Tavern, which had boasted the biggest bar in England, had been demolished and replaced by a much smaller public house and some shops. The other large public house had also gone.

'I was only really concerned about one thing in going back,' he said, *'and that was the verse, "A prophet is not without honour except in his own country." I wondered if returning there would be difficult. But from the very beginning, we were well received in the Centre and at*

the doors. We had 4½ good years of ministry there. The focus of my ministry was to provide, in Howard Hall, a place where people could come in and find a community spirit based upon gospel preaching. As well as door-to-door work, we had a full programme of activities. These included: Just Looking, where we studied a passage from the Bible and enjoyed a cup of tea; club nights for young people; a weekly Bible Study; the Mums and Tots Group; a 16+ Group and a Men's Meeting, not to mention our regular Sunday service and Sunday School. We also restarted the Ladies' Meeting that had not functioned for a while. In short, we ran a traditional Christian Centre.'

The work in Downham continues today with three missionaries based in the Christian Centre. They have been called from very different backgrounds to serve on the estate. And, faithful to their calling as those who have gone before, they are befriending the people they meet in the hope that they can introduce them to Jesus Christ.

Hooligans and others

Much of the work done in Downham, from the 1950s onwards, involved young people. The London City Mission has worked with children from before the days of Ragged Schools. In the indices of the society's magazines, you can trace the articles written specifically about youth work, as well as stories about individual children. Apart from accounts relating to Ragged Schools, they first appeared in 1882 headed, 'Mission to Post-Office and Telegraph Boys'. Between then and the outbreak of World War I there were occasional articles about specific groups, identified either by their jobs or their problems. We have them on an orphan working school (1885), telegraph boys (1898), stable boys on the Strand and Fleet Street (1889), the children of the monkey boats (1900) and rough lads in South London (1903). In the early years of the 20th century a new term – 'hooligans' – came into common use, and the LCM used it extensively. Such youngsters seem to have weighed on the mind of one LCM supporter in particular. '*The Society's kind friend at Forest Hill ... has erected a Drill Hall (to be used also for Mission purposes) for rough lads, and a cottage for the Missionary who is to train them.*' In those days militaristic training, such as the boys would have received in their new drill hall, did not seem out of place in a Christian context. Dealing with hooligans features in articles in both 1910 and 1913. With the end of World War I it seems that children in general, rather than particular groups, became a focus of attention. So we find that children's evangelism is featured (1921), as are young people and revolutionary doctrines (1926), the younger generation (1926), the Bible and youth (1927), Crusade for youth (1929) and the Boys' Brigade (1933).

World War II seems to have changed the focus again. Mission to young people is more often featured in the Magazine. There are reports of thriving youth ministries. '*The missionaries are reporting progressive youth work. There are ten thousand children in our Sunday Schools and crowds of young people who are learning to live and work for Jesus.*' In Stratford the hall was crowded with young people, and the missionary ran five 'clans' of Campaigners. In South London 120 young people attended a Mission Hall's youth organisations, most from homes with no church connection. The Mission Hall in Tottenham had a Bible class of 60. And, '*Youth Rallies held in connection with the Society's halls are revealing a wealth of spiritual power ... In Leyton recently ... 250 young people were present.*'

In the 1950s up to 900 children and young people would meet annually in the Mission's Headquarters – the noise can only be imagined! – for a Youth Rally in connection with 'The Messenger', an evangelistic magazine which was then distributed to 30,000 London homes. Many of the young folk were avid readers of the children's page and a number had come to collect competition prizes. A film, 'Travels through the Holy Land' was shown and the meeting had a profound affect on the missionaries who ran it. *'We caught a vision of thousands of London homes – homes where sin and sorrow spoil the happiness and comfort of little children; we saw the glorious possibilities of reaching thousands of pagan parents through converted boys and girls. We could only pray as they left for North, East, South and West, that they would become messengers of God's marvellous light.'*

Hard lessons

The children at that youth rally may or may not have been captivated by a film on the Holy Land, but the teenagers on the streets presented missionaries, especially the older ones, with something of a steep learning curve. On entering a youth club he had been invited to visit, one missionary realised that he might have been better to find out more before going. However, his short address got a good hearing. *'I moved from one to another, trying to make them feel at home with me, to relax and tell me something about themselves ... G. worked at a welding plant, was eighteen years of age, but earned only £4. ... I veered round to my sermon, and spoke quite pointedly for a moment or two, then asked them, "What do you hope to do with your life?" "We want to form a musical group, good stuff you know, not this rock 'n roll, but real good music like traditional jazz ... I'm saving up for a trumpet, then we shall be going all out to get to the top." Here was ambition, diligence and determination which I could not help admiring while deploring that it was not being expended on some more worthy object.'*

The London City Mission's work with the children and young people who came to its Mission Halls expanded and diversified through the 1950s. Traditional Sunday Schools, Bible Classes and Youth Fellowships attracted some, youth clubs and sports and games brought others. In the following years, with youth culture rapidly changing around them, missionaries also became involved in school assembles. By 1977 one was in school three days a week, the headmistress being happier that Religious Education was taught by someone who had a faith rather than a press-ganged teacher who did not. The LCM ran houseparties for the young, then camps, during which numbers of those who attended came to personal faith in Jesus. New ways were always being sought for presenting the gospel to a generation whose attention span seemed to diminish by the year. While most work was done with groups of children, some ministries lent themselves to individual work. When a missionary took the puppets with which he told the Christmas story to a hospital, he met with wards full of children, and with one or two individually. *'The hospital chaplain asked me to show my puppet ... to a young patient of 14 who had sustained severe head injuries. Apparently, he was not responding to the world outside himself ... I placed my puppet close to him and he began to pat its head and then gave it a long loving embrace ... I spoke to a Down's syndrome teenager who was dying of cancer. His family had deserted him, but God hadn't. He loved the Lord Jesus and sang a Christian song to me. He has since died and gone to be with the Lord.'*

The birth of the Youth Department

By the 1970s, the work among young people which had developed through the Fifties and Sixties was in need of new direction, as it sought to adapt to the changing society of the day. Not everyone who is called to be a City Missionary has a natural bent for youth work and not all have a head full of ideas. But there was someone in Headquarters who had both. In 1978 George Hider was invited by the Mission's General Secretary, Duncan Whyte, to establish a Youth Department. His first reaction – and it remained with him for several months – was that the LCM was too old to take on that kind of commitment; that an organisation with such a history would not be flexible enough to accommodate the programmes he knew would be necessary. But for the next eight years, George came up with idea after idea and the Mission ran with them. He held holiday clubs in Mission Halls, churches and schools, both to reach children and to train others in youth work. Young Christians were encouraged to attend houseparties, sometimes as many as 100 at a time, and camps too. Youth Alive weekends, with 20 to 40 teenagers, gave a tightly packed programme of teaching as well as experience in practical evangelism. The gap year scheme, initially known as 'Voluntary Evangelism' or 'VE', which had begun in 1976, was further developed. Many of the young men and women who formed those early teams have since moved on into full-time Christian ministry, insisting that their time with the LCM was formative in the development of their vision and sense of calling. The short-term summer volunteer scheme was also expanded. Each year, as many as a hundred young adults gave a month or two of their time to the Mission. They were used in halls and churches as well as in outreach to tourists. A mobile unit (another of George Hider's ideas) toured the city. From it, two missionaries conducted campaigns and holiday clubs. With a view to the work growing, he arranged training days for missionaries, covering such topics as schools work and the use of modern technology in evangelism. True to his vision, and the vision of the Mission that had the courage to graft a Youth Department on to an old society, the ministry has continued and grown. It is a major feature of the work today.

17

New Age?

'London, thou art the flower of cities all!'
William Dunbar

'London is a modern Babylon.'
Benjamin Disraeli

Between 1900 and 1960 the LCM knew of 76,618 who professed conversion to Christ through its ministries.

1960 – *Lady Chatterley's Lover, by D. H. Lawrence, is declared not to be obscene in terms of the Obscene Publications Act.*
1961 – *The BBC decides to drop Children's Hour because of a diminishing audience.*
1964 – *Mods and Rockers run riot on the South Coast.*
1965 – *A housewife, Mrs Mary Whitehouse, launches her 'Clean Up TV Campaign'.*
1968 – *People living in London's new tower blocks fear for their safety as the 22-storey Ronan Point is badly damaged in a gas explosion.*

'All of the indicators show that the period between 1956 and 1973 witnessed unprecedented rapidity in the fall of Christian religiosity amongst the British people. In most cases, at least half of the overall decline in each indicator recorded during the century was concentrated in those years... Across the board, the British people started to reject the role of religion in their lives – in their marriage, as a place to

baptize their children, as an institution to send their children for Sunday school and church recruitment, and as a place for affiliation...'
Callum G. Brown, *The Death of Christian Britain*

'For the generations growing up since the 1960s, new ethical concerns have emerged to dominate their moral culture — environmentalism, gender and racial equality, nuclear weapons and power, vegetarianism, the well-being of body and mind — issues with which Christianity and the Bible in particular are perceived as being wholly unconcerned and unconnected.'
Callum G. Brown, *ibid*

'How does it feel?
How does it feel
To be on your own
With no direction home
Like a complete unknown
Like a rolling stone?'
Bob Dylan

Old was out; new was in. The Sixties had arrived. New cars, capable of 80 mph, crawled round the streets of London at 15 and new roads were cut through the city to accommodate them. In that decade alone, more people were decanted – that was the 'in' word as it sounded better than saying that their homes were demolished – to accommodate roads than were rendered homeless in the 19th century to make way for London's entire rail system. And these were not the only houses to be torn down. Sound Victorian terraces which, had they been upgraded, would have done good service well into the 21st century, gave way to tower blocks that had to be replaced before the end of the 20th. But they were new in the Sixties, and new meant good.

There was also a new generation. Their parents, brought up during the Depression years of the 1930s, went on to fight in World War II, or stayed at home and coped with the blackout, Blitz, ration books and recycled clothes. The post war baby boom of the mid-to-late Forties produced the children on whom they based their personal hopes and their hope for the nation's bright new future. Having had few treats in the austere years of their own childhood, they scrimped and saved to give their children everything. Parents wanted to provide the next generation with all the opportunities they felt they had lost to the war years, and society as a whole went along with them. Universities and colleges opened their doors to more students every year. Course fees were paid and student grants made it possible, just, for children from even quite poor homes to have further education. Proud parents watched them graduate; the first of their family ever to reach such a goal. They then smiled with satisfaction when their offspring found their first professional jobs and had more on their pay slip at the end of the month than their parents had after 20 years' work. For those who didn't go on to further education there were apprenticeships available and jobs to choose from.

Spend, spend, spend

Young people in the Sixties had money in their pockets, and they didn't want it to stay there for long. They were told that they had 'never had it so good'. Having worn 'hand-me-downs' themselves, mothers encouraged their daughters towards new and fashionable clothes (though they didn't always approve of the results!) and fathers admired their sons' smart suits. The boutique was born and fashion became big business. London's young men headed to Carnaby Street, while their girlfriends shopped in the King's Road, Chelsea. Consumerism was alive and kicking, even if it sometimes had to be fed on the 'never never'. And the residents of many parts of London watched trendy shops open and wondered where their grocer, butcher and baker had moved to.

The LCM's 126th Annual Report (1961) gives a Mission's eye view of what was happening. '*Old slum properties are being replaced by high-storied flats, and families are being thrown together in a vast machinery of modern design, in communities of concrete and steel. Streets are congested with the ceaseless movement of modern transport ... The car and the television are considered to be essential to family life. The general system of hire-purchase monopolises thousands of homes and provides alluring attractions.*' Then it went on to the spiritual condition of society: '*Crime, violence, gangsterism, pornography, sexual abnormalities, dens of vice, strip tease, gambling, drunkenness, dishonesty, are some of the obvious signs of the breakdown in spiritual strongholds. The broken home, illicit relationships, deliberate unbelief, the denial of God's Word, the neglect of God's Day, constitute a stern challenge to the Christian Church.*' And it was a stern challenge to the LCM, too.

Things were changing in ways that affected the day-to-day work of missionaries. Because even more women were out at work missionaries could knock on a streetful of doors and find only a few at home. Even those who were in presented a different challenge. Some were grandmothers looking after their grandchildren to allow their daughters to work, and that's not an ideal situation in which to engage in deep conversations about the soul. And those women who were at home often had the television on. Having switched it on for the children's programmes in the early afternoon, it remained on for the rest of the day. It did not take missionaries long to discover that nothing distracts more easily than a flickering television in the corner of a room, and nothing takes away the thrust of a spiritual conversation more quickly than the immediate change to boxed entertainment. One missionary drew this conclusion, *"If at first you don't succeed, try, try again," and the only way to obtain fruit in this most difficult and discouraging of tasks, is to visit and visit, and visit again, even though one may see no apparent result, relying solely upon the promise of God that in due season we shall reap, if we faint not.'*

In addition to the regular work of their districts, and the workplaces they continued to visit, places of entertainment and sport presented further opportunities and challenges to missionaries. Every June, as race-goers worked out how much they could risk on the horses and dreamed of what they could buy with their winnings, other plans were also being laid. *'Epsom Downs ... provide the background of the world's most notable race, the English Derby, and becomes thronged with people ... It is colourful, lively and creates a mood of pleasurable excitement. People from many countries meet here. Business firms organise parties. Communities send their representatives and thousands of Londoners join the crowds. For this reason City Missionaries are sent to the Downs during this memorable week, to present the claims of Christ and to engage in personal evangelism ... There must of necessity be organisation in racecourse evangelism. So while a group of men conducted open-air meetings, others made their way into caravans, to groups of people and to the gypsies.'* The following year a report on the work at Epsom painted a very different picture. *'Racecourse behaviour is degrading. Drinking demoralises decent citizens; the raucus cries of tipsters and bookmakers are mellowed by the screams of little children. Barking dogs, hilarious girls, industrious beggars, combine to create a noise and squalor.'* Epsom was indeed a mission field, and the LCM was right in the thick of the noise and bustle with the offer of a free salvation.

Hyde Park

Epsom was not the only place for which the LCM made plans for evangelism. Where better to preach the gospel than Hyde Park, the traditional home of the soapbox? While an LCM speaker may have looked as though he was totally spontaneous, it was the kind of spontaneity that came from good planning and preparation. And a glimpse at a planning meeting shows that great things were expected of the work to be done. *'Revival! Regeneration! Redemption! These great words were to be heard frequently during the afternoon while we discussed, planned and anticipated another season's sowing on the fringe of the world's most famous Park ... Sometimes they are met with marked opposition, with the usual observation of the short-coming of religious leaders, but in each case the opportunity is used to bring the personal challenge of the Gospel to bear upon the speaker, with the reminder that "every one of us shall give an account of ourselves to God"'.* When a listener at one Hyde Park meeting commented that there was a difference between the missionaries and others who often spoke, the preacher explained that *'each man can speak from a personal experience of Christ, and we earnestly believe the Bible to be God's Word.'*

Most contacts made at open-air meetings last just for an afternoon, but missionaries often invest much time and effort in relationships with those they meet. One such was Jimmy. He was contacted through that Sixties institution, Radio Luxembourg, and its Bible Gospel Broadcasting Station. The LCM was contacted by the Radio Station when Jimmy claimed to have come to faith. He was unemployed and in need of a suit of clothes and spiritual support. Jimmy got both and much more. The man was helped to find employment, but his drink problem made it hard for him to keep down a job and his situation went from bad to worse. One day, when he opened his door to the missionary, *'He looked haggard; his eyes were bloodshot and there were no bedclothes or mattress on his bed. A couple of ragged bits of carpet covered the wire springs ... I arranged for him to call round at my home late that night ... when he did, I gave him a mattress.'* So it went on, with the missionary going far more than the second mile. And we can sense the man's sadness when he concluded, *'I feel I can no longer help him financially. I call and see him. Pray with him and for him ... May God help him.'*

The Messenger

London has always had its pub culture, and in the Sixties (as at the turn of the 21st century) it had a blossoming café culture. Espressos were the things to be drinking, and Coca Cola had crossed the Atlantic. As they always had done, missionaries went where the people were, into pubs and cafés with their tracts and offer of salvation. Surprisingly publicans were often quite co-operative when it came to allowing them to engage their customers in conversation. At that time the LCM produced a monthly magazine called 'The Messenger', to be used, as we have seen, as a hand-out and as a means of opening conversations. It was edited by F.H. Wrintmore, a gifted missionary who had been moved to the Mission's Headquarters to edit the main LCM Magazine and to supervise the work north of the river. He also wrote poetry and numerous books about the LCM. The contents of one issue of 'The Messenger' give a flavour. Attractively produced for the time and in two colours, it has a photo and text on the front, then two pages of thoughts on the fact that Jesus is the Sovereign God. That is followed by a touching story obviously aimed at women readers, and then the children's page, complete with questions to be answered and sent to Uncle Remus at Headquarters. The remaining three pages discuss the Christian life, the week leading up to Christ's crucifixion and the subject of prayer. 'The Messenger' was just the right size to slip into a jacket pocket or handbag.

Today the contents would be regarded as too heavy to use as a general hand-out, but it has to be remembered that in the Sixties even those who did not come from church-going families still had some knowledge of the Christian faith from school and Sunday school. Not only that, Billy Graham had taken London by storm in the Fifties, and returned in 1966 for another campaign. However, it was difficult for Christian writers steeped in the certainties of the older evangelicalism to relate to the changing mood of society. Christianity was very much in the firing line as the Sixties developed. The Bishop of Woolwich's book *Honest to God* hit the headlines when it questioned traditional Christian teaching, and in 1971 John Lennon was to invite people to *'Imagine... no hell below us, above us only sky..., no religion...nothing to kill or die for.'* Evangelists from Whitefield and Wesley to Billy Graham had been able to assume at least a minimal knowledge of Christianity, and a basic respect for it, among their hearers. The 1960s were something else.

The coin has two sides

Not all of the cafés missionaries visited were clean, nor did all boast new formica-topped tables. *'One café where I have entrance has this notice up:"No young women served". No decent young women would enter there,'* one missionary said, *'for most of the customers are vagrants. At the beginning of the year I purchased tea for all the customers and challenged their souls... My personal contacts in Public Houses and cafés give me entrance to many homes.'* Swinging London in the Sixties was not exciting for everyone. The city had, as always, its underclass. And while the London City Mission was still finding ways of reaching bright young things, it knew how to reach the poorest, too. *'Rain pours into the houses,'* wrote a missionary in 1963, *'The walls are scarred and dilapidated. ... Mr S., a broken, repentant man. His wife ran away with another man and he sought escape in drink and gambling. He had drifted into the depths. But he allows me to read and to pray with him. On one visit he requested that I should hear his own prayer ..."Unto Thee, O Lord, do I lift up my soul. O my God, I trust in thee" ... He has been gloriously restored!'*

That same year many of the poorest of the poor in London were sad to see the retirement of their missionary, 'The Vagrants' Friend'. This man, one of a number of Scots who have served with the LCM, spent long lone nights on London's embankments, and in the dark lanes where homeless people hid themselves from the police. Not long before he retired, in a waiting room in Victoria Station, travellers demanded to know why a smelly tramp should be allowed to share the room with them. The missionary appeared on the scene. Kneeling at the vagrant's feet, he took off the man's broken shoes, wiped his swollen smelly feet, and gave him a new pair of socks. Then he helped the fellow up before taking him to his own home for a bath and a change of clothes. Nearly 40 years later, there are still missionaries who kneel beside the bruised and broken, the homeless and the addicted, to comfort and help them.

London's West End

In London music was particularly big business in the Sixties. Beatlemania hit the city like a storm, and others followed in the Beatles' wake. Performances drew crowds of thousands of screaming fans to the West End. Concerts, plays, shows and musicals became more brash, controversial and popular. The entertainment industry was in the public eye as never before. The LCM did not neglect the people behind the glitz. One missionary's remit was to work in theatres, as well as visiting the city police and caring for the residents around Covent Garden. He never found himself out of a job. His Journal gives some insight into what he did. *'One day I spent forty minutes in the Opera House and another fifty minutes in Leicester Square; I had knocked on about sixty doors in district visitation and had an answer from about twenty English-speaking people.' 'On a Sunday afternoon I made my way down Bow Street and turned into Drury Lane Theatre ... There, sitting on the kerb, was a drunken man. I had my Bible with me, I put it on the kerb and I sat by his side.' 'It is about twenty minutes to ten − I am in the Opera House to meet a few people in the Canteen.' 'A Dance Manager asked me to assist a young woman ... By visitation and prayer I was able to lead her into peace.'* When the crowds arrived, screaming at their favourite stars, the missionary was out with his tracts.

The sound of silence

Slowly, but with increasing speed as the Sixties went on, Britain's industrial base eroded and a service economy began to grow up in its place. By the middle of the decade, Londoners were being hit hard. While Oxford Street was noisy with thousands of shoppers, the docks began to lapse into silence. The Thames, having been the life-blood of London since the first settlement was established, ceased to support the trade for which it had been famed. Container ships were too big to come upriver, and the decrease in British manufacturing industries meant that goods no longer needed to be shipped overseas. The very idea of London docks closing down was so outrageous some did not believe it until it actually began to happen. While there was still a young generation for whom life was good, their fathers were finding out for the first time what it meant to be on the dole.

When patterns of employment change radically, some rethinking has to be done in the LCM. What does it do with workplace missionaries whose docks and industries downsize or cease to function? Since its inception, the London City Mission has lived with change. When horse-drawn cabs went out, the missionary who served the cabbies was moved to reach those who worked with new fangled motor cars. When electricity took over from gas, missionaries moved accordingly. The society has never felt a need to try to perpetuate the past. While some organisations hold on with such tenacity to their original very specific objective rather than seeing where it fits into the big picture, the LCM has tried hard to avoid doing that. So when an industry closed, the missionary who ministered in it was not, like the workers, redundant. There will always be work for missionaries as long as there are people in London.

New legislation

The 1960s brought changes that were exciting, and others that caused Christians deep concern. 1967 saw the passing of the Abortion Act and the Sexual Offences Act that allows for homosexual acts to take place between consenting adults. Morality was changing, life was becoming cheap, and the unspeakable became the topic of conversation. Missionaries had never had their eyes closed to what was happening around them because they lived in the real world. No missionary was hermetically sealed from the declining standards of morality. Nor were they unaware and unaffected by changes in spiritual things. *'I think that in some ways it has taken 30 years for the passing of these two laws to impact on our evangelism, but we are certainly feeling it now,'* says a contemporary missionary. *'Homosexuality and abortion are so widely accepted, even within parts of the church, that conveying Bible truths on sexuality and the sanctity of life makes us seem bigoted. Today it is alright to hold any opinion but belief in the Word of God.'*

The flood of newness ran deep in the Sixties, and for years to come. Behind the passing trends of fashion and music something more fundamental was changing in British society. Where previous generations had concealed their disbelief behind a socially acceptable religion and outward morality, it now became fashionable to denounce historic Christian beliefs and to flout Christian moral values. Disillusioned with the hypocrisies of their elders, many young people experimented idealistically with new beliefs and lifestyles. They founded communes, squatted in empty mansions, travelled to Himalayan valleys to sit at the feet of self-proclaimed gurus, and demonstrated violently, against the war in Vietnam and against every imaginable authority. Church attendance dropped dramatically – so much so, that later historians would point to the Sixties as 'the death of Christian Britain'. A new term entered the language: 'Post-Christian'. With its calling to go to those who would not come to a church, the LCM and its ministry had never been needed more. For the Mission, the challenge was to understand what was happening to the culture, and to continue to love and engage positively with unbelievers, while still proclaiming the unchanging and unique Christian message.

18

Mass Immigration

'*1950s: Continued efforts to rebuild London's industry and infrastructure lead to the encouragement of settlers from Ireland, the Caribbean, South Asia, Italy and Cyprus. Chinese community develops in Soho.*'

'*1970s: Political refugees arrive from Chile, Argentina and other countries. Asians are expelled from Uganda and many also settle in London. Oil crisis sees financial boom in Gulf states which results in Arab investment, and Arab presence, in London. Turkish invasion of part of Cyprus brings refugees to London. Vietnamese refugees begin to arrive.*'

Nick Merriman, (ed.), *The Peopling of London*

'*Local churches in areas where there is a large population from overseas have for the most part been conspicuously ineffective in their outreach, and in the extent to which they have been able to bring members of other social groups into their fellowship.*'

On the Other Side, Evangelical Alliance's Commission on Evangelism, 1968

'*I pity the poor immigrant*
Who wishes he would've stayed home,...
Whose visions in the final end
Must shatter like the glass.
I pity the poor immigrant
When his gladness comes to pass.'

Bob Dylan

'Personal evangelism is still the prime method...
We must be realists, but there is no need to be defeatists. As we move
into the Seventies, we remember that they are years of grace, years of
our Lord. The decisive conflict with evil has already been fought
and won on the Cross and in the tomb.'
On the Other Side, Evangelical Alliance's Commission on
Evangelism, 1968

Between 1900 and 1980, LCM missionaries made over 96 million
visits to houses in the city, and distributed 134 million Bibles,
testaments and tracts.

'The key to India is in London'
Benjamin Disraeli

If the Sixties was a decade of new ideas, the Seventies was one of new people. London had always been a cosmopolitan city, perhaps more so than any other. '*There is hardly such a thing as a pure Englishman in this island. In place of the rather vulgarised and very inaccurate phrase, Anglo-Saxon, our national denomination, to be strictly correct, would be a composite of a dozen national titles*' (*The Times*, 1867, quoted in Roy Porter, *London, a Social History*). It is hard to imagine what even the writer of that article in the mid-19th century would have made of London in the Seventies. At the end of the decade, of London's 6.6 million population, 382,000 were from Europe, 296,000 from Asia, 170,000 from Africa, 168,000 from the Caribbean and 69,000 came from the Mediterranean countries. One in every six of the capital's population was born outside of the United Kingdom. That did not mean that one in six people met on every single city street would be from another country, because immigrants usually congregate together in a few localities. When the 1981 census was taken, '*Brent's population was a third brown and black, and Ealing had wards with over 85 per cent coloured. Blacks have tended to settle near the centre (Notting Hill, Lambeth), while Asians, setting up shops and small businesses, have headed for suburbia, especially west and north-west London*' (ibid).

The wide mouth of the Thames estuary seems to have sucked people in from other countries for as far back as history records. Over the centuries England became a useful refuge in times of political or religious intolerance or economic stress, and London was the obvious place to go – it was the port to which most ships sailed. Some came by invitation, especially members of Commonwealth nations who could come and go freely, and people from countries with which England had trading relations or political alliances. Others perhaps came less willingly, to serve English families – a practice begun in Roman times and continuing today. In the 1950s, West Indians arrived in large numbers, encouraged to come because the transport system was grinding to a halt for lack of staff. Then the Seventies saw the arrival of Kenyan and Ugandan Asians, no longer welcome in their adopted African home but possessing British passports.

Of course, migrants to London were not all from abroad. They came from Shetland in the north, from Anglesey in Wales and the furthest reaches of the Irish coast. The capital city has acted like a magnet to many over the course of its history. Dick Whittington was not the only one to head for the capital. *'In 1707 it was observed that for any son or daughter of an English family that exceeds the rest in beauty, or wit, or perhaps courage, or industry, or any other rare quality, London is their North star"* (quoted in *London, the Biography*, Peter Ackroyd).

The LCM has always seen itself as ministering to everyone who lives in London, whether or not they were born within the sound of Bow Bells. Taking a sample of the LCM Magazine articles from across the decades we discover that missionaries befriended Jewish people (1830s), and incomers from Latin America (1840s), France (1850s), Ireland (1860s), the Orient (1870s), Portugal (1880s), Asia (1890s), Scandinavia (1900s), China (1910s), Russia (1920s), America (1930s), Italy (1940s), the West Indies (1950s), Germany (1960s), Eastern Europe (1970s), overseas students (1980s) and Spain (1990s). As one of today's missionaries, Atsu Tettevi (himself an immigrant from Ghana), said, *'Having prayed that the Lord would involve me in working for the salvation of the world, he took me to London where all the world can be found.'*

One reason so many people groups were contacted through the LCM was that immigrant communities often lived in the poorer parts of the city, the very areas in which the society's men worked. But there was another reason, an altogether higher one. Jesus commissions his disciples – from the 1st to the 21st centuries – with these words: '*All authority in heaven and on earth has been given to me. Therefore go and make disciples of all nations, baptising them in the name of the Father and of the Son and of the Holy Spirit, and teaching them to obey everything I have commanded you.*' And when City Missionaries felt overwhelmed by the enormity of the task, or downcast by rejections, they could remember how the Lord completed their commissioning, '*And surely I am with you always, to the very end of the age*' (Matt. 28:18–20).

While missionaries were well aware of the problems resulting from immigration, they also recognised the opportunities it brought. '*The invasion of London by many thousands of immigrants has introduced patterns of life that could retard our progress. These visitors have brought with them their own religions; their own particular ideologies; their own sense of gregariousness, which has brought to some districts serious overcrowding. Some have also brought systems of violence and moral ugliness. Many live and desire to live – in pockets of isolation. There are, however, other immigrants who are contributing richly to the spiritual life of the metropolis. We have frequently listened to their open-air services and praised their zest and wish to save souls. These friends have much to teach us today. We need them and they need our encouragement.*'

Prayer supporters

When large numbers of immigrants arrived in the Seventies, the London City Mission knew what it was about. It had a long history of reaching out to people from other cultures; people who spoke different languages and who practised unfamiliar religions. Some, when they arrived in the UK, were prepared to investigate Christianity. They went to the Mission rather than have someone from the LCM approach them. One missionary told of a Muslim man who slipped into his Hall on a Sunday evening. There he heard the gospel for the first time, and it spoke to him directly. At the end of the service, the missionary answered his questions. And before the man left the building, he exclaimed, '*Jesus has brought hope, light and joy to my soul.*' The LCM has a host of prayer supporters, both individuals and those who meet in groups, and that man was an answer to their prayers.

Over the history of the society, people have prayed for the work using a prayer diary. In the Seventies it was called the *Daily Remembrancer*. Each day gave a subject for prayer and a Scripture passage to read. Every aspect of the Mission's activities was covered and, in 1973, the work with immigrants appeared nine times, though they would also be prayed for when their home district was remembered. Other prayer points that year included: two missionaries to newsvendors, bookstall work in Petticoat Lane, tracts left in unopened doors and, on Monday 28th May, '*For the workers engaged in the building of our new headquarters.*' The LCM's new home, Nasmith House at 175 Tower Bridge Road, was opened two years later, by Queen Elizabeth, the Queen Mother. It finally replaced the previous permanent Headquarters that had been destroyed in the Blitz.

Newcomers to London presented a challenge to many missionaries but one, at least, was prepared to accept God's provision of a helping hand. In Hyde Park, near Speakers' Corner, he saw a group of followers of Hare Krishna having a picnic and asked if he could join them. They listened to what he had to say and accepted the literature he gave them concerning Christ being the Light of the World and the only way to God. But then he was at a loss as to how to progress. God does not always answer prayers immediately, but he did that day. As the missionary opened his eyes, he saw a young man wearing a badge that read, 'Smile God loves you'. He called the wearer over and the pair of them engaged in a dialogue about their faith that was listened to by their saffron-clad friends. Their interest was aroused, and a profitable conversation followed. Another answer to the prayers of those who used the *Daily Remembrancer?*

Not all contacts with overseas guests, in this case short-term ones, were as positive. In 1975, 14 years before the fall of communism, an LCM missionary was walking in Piccadilly Circus. *'I saw at least 200 people waiting for coaches,'* he wrote in the Nov./Dec. issue of *Span* (as the LCM Magazine had by then been renamed), *'I introduced myself to one of the guides as a London City Missionary, and asked where they came from. "We are from Russia," she said. I asked whether I might be allowed to distribute some portions of Scripture among her countrymen on the following day. "Yes, you can do that," she replied. The next day aided by two others we waited for these Russian people with 300 gospels and tracts. At last the coaches arrived and all those who disembarked accepted our literature. Then after two minutes a man came out of the hotel asking what we were doing. I introduced myself and stated that we were giving out the Word of God. In great consternation he ran back inside the hotel and seized the gospels out of the hands of those who had accepted them. Then he threw them on the pavement at our feet. We picked them up and counted them. Out of the 200 only 22 had gone. Those were the ones which people had hidden in their pockets.'* Other tourists must have got a surprise when they met one missionary at Speakers' Corner. In 1977 he noted that there were more Arab and Persian tourists in the Park than ever before and he distributed over 150 Arabic and Persian Gospels. For most of these people it was the first time they had seen any part of the

Bible in their own language. He was nearly always able to give people a tract in their own tongue – he carried literature in 50 different languages – but occasionally he was caught out.

Not a Christian country

In April, May and June 1977, London was the main venue for the World of Islam Festival sponsored by the British Arts Council and the British Museum. By then one million Muslims lived in the United Kingdom, not all of them from an Islamic background because British nationals were being converted to Islam. Reaching Muslims was not easy, as many missionaries discovered, especially because they have strict codes by which they live, such as abstaining from alcohol, and they perceive that our 'Christian society' allows for very lax living. When approached, one Muslim man told an LCM missionary, *'Judging by what I have seen, Christians are drunkards and adulterers. You would do well to restrict your missionary operations to your own countrymen.'*

By the end of the 1970s the racial mix in London was such that an article in *Span* was entitled 'Black and White City'. The West London area in which the writer worked was a mix of native British and people from the West Indies, Turkey, Greece and Asia, with small pockets of others from a wide variety of places. The variety was typical though the predominant people groups were different in other parts of the city. More and more of LCM's missionaries found themselves working in racially mixed areas because that was London as it entered the Eighties.

As ever more nationalities were in evidence in the streets of London, the LCM appealed to its supporters to pray quite specifically that God would send missionaries from different ethnic groups, able to speak different languages and to reach out to them with the gospel. He answered in a quite remarkable way, and has done ever since. At the time of writing, about 20 per cent of those serving with the mission come from outside the United Kingdom. Australia, Liberia, Sweden, South Africa, The Netherlands, Zimbabwe, Poland, Uganda, India, Pakistan, Spain, Romania, Guyana, Egypt, Peru, Mauritius, Ghana, America, Germany and the Republic of Ireland are all represented in its ranks. Over 20 languages are spoken by missionaries, and several are converts from Islam and Hinduism, well-equipped to understand the mind-set of those they minister to.

Today all of the LCM's districts are multi-ethnic, some more so than others. In the Borough of Tower Hamlets, which is home to London's largest Bangladeshi community, an LCM team runs *Café Forever*, which is well used by those who live locally. An after-school club with Internet facilities is provided, and (as people in a Muslim community are used to public readings of the Koran) public Bible Readings are held. In such ways the LCM seeks to adapt itself to the communities in which it works. The language skills of missionaries enable some to run courses in English as a second language, and others have drop-in centres where people who are struggling with formal documents, letters, and forms can have help with translation.

19
Women in Mission

'Mr Pearson ... has long seen that some womanly teaching among the women, and especially as connected with a Bible Mission, would be of great assistance to him with regard to his own work ... By the aid of his experience the good woman, Martha, was selected ... Martha's own full experience of poverty fits her to sympathise at once with her poorest neighbours.'
The LCM Magazine, Nov. 1860

'The Mothers' Meeting is conducted by my wife, and there is an average attendance of 80 out of a membership of 120 ... Low, drunken women have signed the pledge, which means cleaner, brighter homes, more food for the children, and more comfort for the husbands, which tends to keep them at home.'
The LCM Magazine, Nov. 1905

'An old lady of eighty-five, living in alms-houses, has forwarded two shillings' worth (of pennies) by the missionary who, nearly thirty years ago, led her to the Lord.'
The LCM Magazine, Aug. 1938

'After spending three weeks in London with LCM, I had a chance to figure out my strengths and weaknesses, and to do all sorts of things that I had never tried before. It was extremely tough at times, and fun at other times, but physically exhausting!'
Patricia Marby, The LCM Magazine, Jan./Feb. 1981

By the beginning of the 1980s, over two and a half thousand missionaries had served with the London City Mission. Some spent their entire career with the LCM, others a shorter period, and a number left and then returned. All were men. But times were changing and the role of women was changing too. Had the time come for women to serve as City Missionaries? The debate went on throughout the Eighties. Eventually the Committee reached its decision, and in 1989 the first woman was accepted as a probationer.

Although women were not appointed as missionaries until so recently, they had been heavily involved in the work of the London City Mission since its inception. Broadly speaking, this was either as supporters, enabling the ministries of the Mission to continue, or as helpers, working in those ministries alongside the missionaries.

Women supporters

From the earliest days of the LCM, women were prominent in raising funds to support missionaries. In 1849 one was responsible for the appointment of eight missionaries. On a visit to Europe the woman, who chose to remain anonymous, became very aware of the blessings God had poured out on England. As a thank-offering for his goodness, she sent a donation of £1,000 to the LCM because she believed that it was, *the most efficient instrument in bringing home to the masses of our population the way of salvation*. Her letter as well as her gift must have been a great encouragement, as she went on to say that, *my confidence in this Society arises entirely from my knowledge of the high standard of character which is maintained in the selection of missionaries.*

Other wealthy women, including a duchess or two, formed 'Ladies Associations' throughout Britain which adopted particular districts of the capital and funded the work. Some held Drawing Room gatherings for their wealthy friends and neighbours. Working parties supplied goods for sales of work, and gardens produced fruit, vegetables and flowers. Some found ingenious ways of helping, and raised a few eyebrows at the same time. A Mrs Puckle, in 1877, wrote to a missionary asking him to collect flowers for the poor from Waterloo Station. The flowers, 60 bunches each with a text attached, duly arrived in a nice basket. *'The people were very much surprised,'* the missionary noted. *'Some asked if I was going to sell them.'* He distributed the flowers around his district, with bunches even going to the men at the local coal depot. One of the coalies, a drunkard, took the flowers home to his wife. The text and flowers made such an impression that the couple started attending church! Women funded the building of some Mission Halls, held sales of work, quietly gave money for the relief of individual needs, or left legacies to the LCM when they died.

Such helpers took a detailed and prayerful interest in the Mission's work, attending local and national annual meetings, and reading carefully the reports in the Magazine and in numerous other LCM publications – such as that of the conversion of a rather special woman, Mrs. Caroline Merriott, in 1925. Caroline, who was to live for more than ten years as a Christian, was a hundred years old at her conversion. *'Isn't it wonderful that I should wait till I am one hundred before coming to the Lord Jesus,'* she told a missionary. *'Wonderful,'* he noted, *'but risky!'*

With or without women workers, the LCM owed a great deal to women!

Women workers

Women did much more than provide the financial support, however. Missionary after missionary would testify that they were only able to carry on their work because of the devoted help of the women who worked alongside them as volunteers. Chapter nine described the lending-library run in Poplar by John Galt's female helpers. The missionaries in the docks relied on women to provide the teas and the welcome at 'The Stranger's Rest' laid on for foreign sailors, and we have also seen the similar work done for soldiers.

Others staffed the Ragged Schools that many missionaries organised for the poorest children in their districts. Sunday Schools also made use of women's gifts. A few, like Mary Carpenter, used their considerable energy and influence to effect change. Not only was she involved in both Ragged Schools and Sunday Schools, she also pushed for parliamentary recognition of the reformatories and industrial schools that evangelicals were setting up for street children.

In 1859 the new missionary to Willesden discovered that because the local vicar did not have a curate to support him, pastoral visiting would have been sadly neglected had it not been for several 'pious ladies' who did what the vicar was unable to do. The missionary had the good grace to note that their labours did much to smooth his way. Around that time the London Female Bible and Domestic Mission appointed Bible-women to needy parts of London, and because LCM missionaries also served such areas there might have been tensions. However, the women were charged with supplying the very poorest of the population with copies of the Bible, and with teaching them how to look after themselves and others, and in practice Bible-women and missionaries complemented each other. It was noted that, '*females are* evidently *the more qualified persons to teach the women whom they visit how to cook, to scour the floors, to rear babies, and other like domestic and household duties.'* These women had access where men had not. Some women, who were so ashamed of their poor homes that they would not let a clergyman or missionary in, opened their doors to women.

Women missionaries?

In 1861, so well were Bible-women received, that the London City Mission debated at some length the possibility of employing women to labour alongside the men. After long and serious consideration, it was decided that the work of Bible-women and missionaries were best kept apart and administered by separate agencies, although they should continue to co-operate with each other. One fear underlying this decision was that the City Mission would come to be seen as 'women's work', and the supply of male recruits would dry up. Yet a publication entitled, 'Women's Work in the Church of Christ' stated, '*When the heart of a woman has been won to the love of Christ, it is her happiness, her delight, to be employed in works of mercy. The truth of this is attested by the large number of voluntary workers among us.*' Nor were these women all wealthy do-gooders. On the subject of finance, the article says, '*Let those who can give their services at their own expense, do so: and those who cannot, receive the proper remuneration.*' The LCM endorsed the sentiment by republishing the article in its magazine.

The London City Mission always had another group of women workers – missionaries' wives. In 1886, in St. Martin's Hall, Long Acre, a meeting was held for missionaries and their wives. (Unmarried missionaries were allowed to take a sister.) The hall was full and tea was served, after which the Chairman, on behalf of himself *and his wife*, addressed the assembly. '*I* have the happiness of knowing the immense power for good that a good wife possesses,' he told them, 'and I would humbly suggest ... that if the wife's heart is in the work of the husband, then there will be united prayer, and there will be great blessing in answer to that united prayer, and the important work of this most excellent Institution will, therefore, be greatly extended and furthered.' One wife ran a women's meeting with a membership of 120. And this was no social afternoon; it was as much a gospel meeting as those organised by her husband. Those who attended were an interesting mix; they included a flower seller, a sandbag maker, a haddock cleaner, a matchbox maker and two Jewesses who begged to be admitted because they liked hearing the Gospel. Women were converted through that wife's preaching and many signed the pledge. One woman, who had been the terror of the neighbourhood, came, was converted and brought along her drunken friends. Many of the missionaries' wives had preaching and pastoral ministries among the women of their district. Fredrick Robinson was missionary to the Tabard Street District of Southwark in 1912. His journal reveals a ministry that was very much a team effort with his wife:

'With my wife and another Missionary, conducted a large meeting at the Assembly Hall, Mile End... On a Sunday evening, the open-air service was progressing very happily when there was a rush and a scream. Two women and two men were in fierce conflict; blows from fists and iron bars were followed by the flow of blood. I carried on with the open-air meeting and my wife walked over to the woman who was the ringleader of the fight, linking her arm and took her for a little walk, thus stopping the fierce fight. The police said it was neatly done and at great personal risk and courage...

'A man called today to see Mrs Robinson. Would she visit 47, —— Road? He said his wife was strange in the mind... Visited today in ——Street. I was called on to visit a man in his home and was glad *that my wife accompanied me. I had to speak to the man (who was an embezzler) in a way that I have perhaps never spoken before; and my wife was equally plain with the woman.'*

Noisy but needed

Women volunteers and missionaries' wives have always played a major part in the children's work at Mission Halls and Christian Centres. The Ragged Schools of early years have been succeeded by the holiday clubs, football teams, youth groups and after-school clubs of today. Then there are the children's camps. By the mid-1970s camps were a feature of the LCM's summer programme and the helpers were not all Londoners. The woman school teacher from Yorkshire, who upped sticks at the end of term and helped with a camp in Norfolk in 1975, was just one of the hundreds of leaders who have given their spare evenings and holiday time to the Mission's work with young people. While camps are great fun (and very hard work!), they can have eternal consequences. The report of the 1975 camps concluded, *'Children's Camps will always be costly in time and effort, calling for much patience and involvement by the workers, but the joy of seeing young people opening their hearts to the Saviour and committing their lives to Him will always make it time well spent and infinitely worthwhile.'*

From 1976 the Voluntary Evangelism Scheme offered young women as well as men training in gospel outreach and front-line experience working alongside missionaries for a year. These young workers were not paid, but they were accommodated, fed and given pocket money. In the main, they served as part of the staff at Christian Centres. After their year, some stayed for a second year, while several were recruited and paid from locally raised funds to continue their work in a particular centre.

In such ways, the LCM became used to the idea of women working as members of the full-time team.

Shorter periods of service were also offered. One of them, the Summer Evangelism Scheme, started in 1977, gave young people aged 17 plus the opportunity to get a brief taste of working with the Mission. *'I found the door-to-door visitation in Hoxton a most valuable experience. I had never tried anything like that before and it was a time of totally relying on God for the words and guidance. The open-air evangelism at Tower Hill was certainly an eye opener... The overall impression I got was one of a harvest field in the city with a great need for the work that the LCM does.'*

First, but not the first

When, after all this, in 1989 the first woman was accepted as a salaried 'woman evangelist', she was by no means the first to be doing the work of the City Mission. *Span* marked the occasion. *'This issue of the Mission's magazine is somewhat unique in that for the first time since 1835, it features the work of an LCM full-time lady worker ... The first successful candidate ... was accepted in 1989. She was an excellent candidate, for already she had worked under the supervision of a city missionary ... for 3½ years... Assigned last November to Paget Memorial Hall, King's Cross, after completing a two months' probationary period, she is part of a team consisting of two city missionaries and one or two Voluntary Evangelists.'*

Of course, compared to most Christian Missions the LCM was extraordinarily slow to appoint women as missionaries. It was doubly unfortunate that the question was delayed until the 1980s because, by then, the Church of England was enmeshed in the debate about 'women's ordination' and sensitivities on the issue were heightened in all Christian circles. The Mission's difficulty was compounded by the diversity of views held by Evangelicals. Although it was raised at the same time as that of women's ordination in the Church, there was no connection between the two questions. The LCM has always insisted that the Mission is in no sense a Church or a denomination. It has also stressed that "missionaries" are not to be thought of as ordained ministers. Early missionaries were called 'lay agents', and the Mission boasted in its Magazine that it had pioneered 'lay ministry' in Christian work. When Mission Halls and Christian Centres were hired or built, it was again stressed that these are not churches. They may have a meeting on a Sunday, but they are not allowed to celebrate baptism or the Lord's Supper, and there is no 'membership'. Even the preaching was strictly 'non-ministerial' – a regulation of 1849 told missionaries not to preach 'sermons with three points', but simply to read through a Scripture passage and explain its meaning. So (as the Mission itself recognised in its early days) there was no Biblical or ecclesiastical reason why women should not use their gifts as 'lay agents' alongside men. It should have been a purely pragmatic issue. In the turbulent ecclesiastical climate of the 1980s this basic fact was not always kept in view.

Since 1988, women missionaries have become an accepted and valued part of the LCM's ministry, using their wide variety of gifts alongside those of their male colleagues. The same spiritual qualifications, the same training period, and the same working patterns are common to all. By the end of the century 32 women had been accepted by the LCM to join the ranks of City Missionaries, among them a missionary's widow, who had served for 36 years as an active wife before going, with flying colours, through all the selection and training process when she applied to serve as a missionary. Already, the term 'woman evangelist' has largely been abandoned as all the LCM's staff carry on the work of personal evangelism by word and deed.

20

Towards a New Millennium

Total of men and women who served as LCM evangelists between 1900 and 1999: 1,183.

'As a rule, those who undertake missionary work have themselves found a religious anchorage, and ardently wish that others should share it... The active virtue of missions lies in their enthusiasm, and the corresponding fault is exaggeration. Principles and expectations differ but enthusiastic zeal and exaggerated language are common to all...'
Charles Booth, 1902

'Over 60 widows and mothers of murdered Royal Ulster Constabulary (were) brought to London as the guests of the City of London police force... On the Sunday morning a conference hall was set aside in their hotel for a service which was conducted by Lionel Ball, Missionary to City of London police...We count it a great privilege to minister, if only in so small a way, to those who have so tragically lost loved ones.'
Span, January 1986

Secretaries and General Secretaries of the London City Mission

(various titles were used, and there was a dual office from 1844 until 1918)

David Nasmith	1835–1837
Rev. John Garwood	1837–1876
Rev. Robert Ainslie	1837–1844
Rev. John Robinson	1845–1876
Rev. Josiah Miller	1876–1880
Rev. J. P. A. Fletcher	1877–1881
Rev. Robert Dawson	1881–1906
Rev. T. S. Hutchinson	1882–1918
Rev. Martin Anstey	1906–1918
Rev. W. P. Cartwright	1918–1951
Rev. Canon C. E. Arnold	1951–1967
Rev. Duncan Whyte	1967–1992
Rev. James McAllen	1992–

'Social problems appear to beset us as never before: the rape of the countryside; inner-city decay; the decline in traditional moral values; rampant materialism; the persistence of gross inequalities in life-chances; the welfare state struggling to meet increasing demands with decreasing hopes of satisfying them; demoralization among educators...; and a general loss of national direction and confidence.'
Edward Royle, *Modern Britain – A Social History, 1750–1985*, 1987

As the 1990s drew on, the LCM was well into its fourth half-century. The 150th anniversary had been marked in 1985, with a celebration in the Royal Albert Hall, attended by over 5,000, with Luis Palau as the special speaker. A commemorative vinyl LP had been issued. By the end of the Nineties, the Mission was issuing CDs. Throughout its life, the society has managed to maintain a steady continuity in its essential work (perhaps undergirded by the longevity of many of its General Secretaries in the job) while having the confidence to adapt and to adopt new methods and ministries.

For many years the first Wednesday of every month has seen the entire Mission staff gathering at Nasmith House for what is called Divisional Day, or 'Divi Day' for short. The name derives from the old system which grouped the missionaries into four geographical 'divisions'. Each of these came to Headquarters on a different day once a month, to hand in their Journals and to receive their pay, in cash (and in strict order of seniority!). While much has changed, the name has survived – although latterly all the missionaries come on the same day, and banked pay slips have replaced the cash. The main element of the day is a meeting of worship and prayer. The singing is stirring and the prayers are fervent and wide-ranging. The meeting concludes with a sermon, usually from the General Secretary. Then there is much talking and fellowship over lunch – possibly taken in the park that surrounds Nasmith House, or perhaps in the local café, the 'Cat and Cucumber', beloved of generations of missionaries for its wonderfully unhealthy menu. Doubtless, missionaries have their differences, but Divi Day sees them at their best, glad to be together and eager to catch up with what is happening in different parts of the city.

Men of previous generations, could they return to share in a modern Divi Day, would undoubtedly notice several obvious changes in addition to the presence of women missionaries and the young people on the 'City Vision' scheme. If they were veterans of a century ago, they would note with concern that the 500 missionaries of the 1890s had only about 150 successors, though veterans from the 1940s and 1950s would feel that the numbers had stayed fairly steady overall. They might be surprised to hear the members of the Executive, even the General Secretary, called by their first names. And the informality of attire would be in sharp contrast to the old days of suits, white shirts and whichever hat (homberg, trilby, or straw boater) was the accepted style of their era. (Not so long ago senior missionaries would ensure that newcomers were given the address of a good laundry where they could have their shirts washed and collars starched!)

Training

Another change, developed during the 1990s, saw most Divi Days as times of in-service training for the whole team. The LCM has always provided on-the-job, apprenticeship training for its new recruits, placing them under the wing of an experienced missionary, and adding lectures at Headquarters. In that way, classroom teaching is immediately put to the test on the streets, while problems encountered on the streets can be brought straight back to the classroom. Because today's city is so amazingly diverse, and so constantly changing, no missionary can afford to stop learning when the initial training is finished – hence the use of Divi Day for a wide variety of lectures, seminars and workshops, dealing with everything from Addiction to Zoroastrianism! There was a time when 'City Missionary' was looked down upon as a second-rate calling, suitable for those who were not gifted enough to become pastors or vicars. That was never an assessment that could stand up to Biblical scrutiny, but it is especially invalid today. Many of the LCM's recent recruits have degrees, in subjects ranging from theology to social work, education to management. But, whatever academic qualifications they have, the LCM looks to make them into 'reflective practitioners of mission', doing the work and thoughtfully assessing what they do.

Behind such visible changes to Divi Days, the old-timers might discover that other significant developments have occurred in the Mission's more recent past. Perhaps the most significant of all has been the trend to man Christian Centres with teams of full-time workers, rather than each being run by a single missionary as was previously the case. Some Centres now have three or even four missionaries and 'City Vision' workers. In part, this reflects the diminishing number of volunteers willing to help run the activities, but, more positively, it is an acknowledgement of the importance of team-work and fellowship in sustaining a tough ministry. It also has the advantage of increasing the number and diversity of the talents and giftings that can be used in a Centre's work.

New ministries

Trying to make full use of the gifts of its staff, the LCM has continued to open up new areas of ministry. By the 1990s New Age thinking was becoming more than just a fringe interest, and the Mission took up the challenge. Paul James-Griffiths started going to the markets and side streets where New Age shops and devotees are to be found: *'We have a bookstall on Neal Street ... Amongst the usual browsers and tourists are many "New Agers" who are seeking healing and enlightenment through a vast array of spiritualities ... We set up our stall in such a way as to attract people to look at the booklets written by Christians. They deal with subjects such as angels, spirit guides, UFOs, psychic readings, astrology, yoga and reincarnation. As we engage people in conversation we share the Gospel with them.'*

New Agers tend to be young, but the population in the United Kingdom is an ageing one. By the turn of the millennium, for the first time since records began, there were more people over 60 years of age than children under 16. That, too, opened up new emphases in ministry, with at least three missionaries spending much of their time visiting residential units for the elderly. George Zammit worked for some years as a missionary in Bermondsey, where he *'first met Doris while presenting an activity at Bermondsey Care Home. Doris had been a very private person and had isolated herself until her circumstances obliged her to move into the Home, but there she became an active participant in the group ... There were opportunities to share God's Word and pray for Doris ... George and his wife Yvonne took Doris to an evangelistic meeting at his church. Doris heard a clear presentation of the Gospel and gave her life to Christ.'*

With his 'Capital Kids' scheme, Phil Moore, the LCM's Youth Director, began using the skills and gifts of missionaries and City Vision volunteers to provide two and three days of intensive children's activities at churches and Christian groups, so encouraging others to develop their work among children.

When the Peabody Trust wanted to redevelop their Covent Garden site, the LCM saw another opportunity and used it. Because the Mission had a long lease for part of the site, the Trust agreed to provide the LCM with accommodation for a bookshop, meeting room and coffee bar. *'Once a run-down area, Covent Garden is now bursting with life from hundreds of boutiques, thousands of visitors and continuous street entertainment ... The aim of the Centre is to reach the drifting, seeking young people who crowd the streets, visiting the music shops, clothes boutiques and New Age outlets. Here in the heart of London's West End, behind the façade of glamour and affluence, are some of the neediest people – spiritually and materially – in our country today.'* 'The Vine' (as the coffee-shop is known) opened in 1998 and has already been the venue for many valuable and even life-changing conversations.

The missionaries who run such ministries are all funded by the LCM, which still depends for its support on donations from individuals and individual churches throughout Britain and Ireland – and even further afield. While few can ever have become City Missionaries for the sake of the pay, the Mission does house all its staff, and the 1990s witnessed the inauguration of a new and sturdy pension scheme. With a new word, 'stress', entering popular culture, the Mission also strengthened its pastoral support of its staff by the appointment of Missionary Superintendents – senior working missionaries who keep an eye on their younger and less experienced colleagues and who are available as a first call in times of trouble.

Amid all that has changed, Divi Days also stand as a reminder of all that is unchanging. The times of prayer deal with the needs of individual districts and people, and of the missionaries who go out to them. The emphasis on prayer underlines the Mission's continuing awareness of those first 'Instructions to Missionaries' (see chapter 3) which urged them to *'go to your District in a spirit of prayer'*. And the Biblical, gospel preaching on those days is in full accord with a further urging of those same 'Instructions': *'Keep the Lord Jesus Christ continually before your own mind, and commend Him and His great salvation to the people...'*

As month succeeded month and the new millennium approached, *Span* revealed how the LCM was still changing people's lives just as when it began 160 years before:

When Kemi, a young Nigerian student, opened the door to find a missionary there, she had no idea that a new life was about to open out in front of her. She accepted some Christian literature and an invitation to attend her local Christian Centre the following Sunday. Over time she made a commitment to Christ and began telling her fellow students about her Saviour. Kemi soon introduced her friend Nkem to Jesus.

Sarah was much in need of support when a missionary knocked on her door to wish her a Happy Easter. He was invited in, and before long she was able to pour out her heart to her sympathetic visitor. *'She had experienced much sadness in her life,'* the missionary said, *'but she still believed in God, and has since become a frequent worshipper at the church. It has been good to call on Sarah fairly frequently ... we often look at passages in the Bible together.'*

It was after he moved to a new area that 12-year-old Daniel began attending meetings in his local Christian Centre. One evening, after a challenging talk at the youth club, he stayed to discuss things further with the missionary. *'He asked if I would like to become a Christian and I did not know what to say ... But then I quickly replied, "I would like to be a Christian." I expressed a simple prayer and the Lord, in that moment, came into my life ... It all seemed so unspectacular, but later proved to be the most significant step in my life.'*

As the year 2000 dawned, James McAllen, the LCM's current General Secretary reflected on the times, on the current state of London, and on the LCM's role.

'History is about God's deeds. Like every story, it has a beginning, a middle and an end. It is God who moves everything towards a goal, a definite point which He has fixed.

'History is also the story of man and his attempt to manage without God. It is a sad story... Mankind has achieved many wonderful things, but ... the rejection of God and the loss of the eternal dimension shuts humanity into a cycle of despair and self-destruction. It happened in Ancient Greece. It is happening in London today...(where we see) the despair of the marginalised, particularly the children, the innocent victims of social disintegration. It was such conditions in the 19th century which led David Nasmith to establish City Missions.

'So what of the 21st century? What remedy do we have for the ills of London? The answer could best be summed up in words from Jeremiah 6:16 –"Stand at the crossroads and look; ask for the ancient paths, ask where the good way is, and walk in it, and you will find rest for your souls."

'All human remedies are bound to fail. They are the product of those whose horizons are limited. God's remedy, on the other hand, is ever new. The Gospel does not date.'

21

Looking Forward

'Research out today reveals that more than 300 languages are spoken by children in London schools, making the capital the most linguistically diverse city on the planet.'
Evening Standard, 21 January 2000

'A housing estate in west London "...really doesn't seem that bad, but if you went inside these places, man, you'd see a different story, and to me that says so much about Britain — the dark things which go on beneath a calm façade." The "dark things" to which he is referring ... are crack-dealing ("there are loads of crack-houses here"); guns ("14-year-olds have them"); and organised crime...'
Author Courttia Newland, who grew up in west London
(in a newspaper interview, April 1997)

'53 per cent of children in Inner London are living in poverty — the highest incidence in Great Britain.'
Greater London Authority, November 2002

'The ten most densely populated districts in Britain are all London boroughs.'
2001 Census figures

'Unemployment figures (2000/2001)
National average: 5.4%
Inner London: 9.5%
Bangladeshis in London: 25%
Black Caribbeans in London: 15.7%'
Greater London Authority, November 2002

'We may live in the age of freedom, but it should more properly be described as the age of selfishness... We live in a world of increasing impermanence, transience and ephemerality, where little or nothing is forever, and individual gratification is the highest priority.'
Martin Jacques, *The Guardian*, 5 October 2002

'Anglican Church "in meltdown" as attendances fall'
Headline, *The Times*, 30 October 2002

The new millennium was just a few months old when a ten-year-old boy was murdered on the North Peckham estate in south London. The tragic death of the young Nigerian immigrant led to a brief flurry of dramatic press reports on the problems of the inner-city. *'A terrible place to die. And a terrible place to live'*, pronounced the headline in *The Independent* over an article which went on to describe the estate: *'Built in 1968, (it) had decayed until it became a byword for inner-city deprivation, a place that was chosen to launch a nationwide urban regeneration scheme.... (It) is an urban sprawl reeking of neglect. Crime, in varying degrees, is ever present... Drug dealing and drug taking are endemic. Demolition workers who have spent eight weeks knocking down about two-thirds of the estate have found 20,000 hypodermic needles and are required always to wear protective gloves.'* Other residents of Peckham protested about 'sensationalist press coverage' that characterised the whole area as a 'war zone', but the fact that other local neighbourhoods are pleasant and peaceful does not imply that 'sink estates' do not exist.

Still needed?

'Exclusions' of difficult children from inner-London schools are running at twice the national average. Juvenile crime is a major problem, with a 40 per cent rise in London street crime reported between April 2000 and January 2001. The Health Service complains of under-funding and tuberculosis is re-appearing with disturbing frequency in many poorer districts. Child abuse cases seem to recur with alarming regularity despite detailed reports and increased legislation. Blackshirt riots, cholera epidemics, and attacks by Zeppelins or V2s sound as remote as a Tolkein fantasy. Levels of prosperity, welfare, social care and health are undoubtedly much improved. Yet, London has multiple problems that are essentially similar to those of earlier centuries, however different their form may be.

The term 'rookery' may be unknown today, but everyone knows of the problem of the tower-blocks, with parts of Shadwell the most over crowded in the European Union. No-one dies of starvation today – but a 1998 report by Sir Donald Acheson described 'food deserts' where the lack of supermarkets and the demise of local small shops means that few fresh foods are available. Acheson concluded, *'Hunger is once again stalking the streets of Britain and is threatening the health of future generations.'* Modern London has its own 'dark heart'.

When we turn to the religious scene, there is still every evidence of profound spiritual need. London's Black-led churches have grown appreciably, largely fuelled by immigration from Africa and the Caribbean, but most denominations are in decline. Between 1979 and 1998, London's church attendance fell by about 11 per cent. Well below 10 per cent of Londoners attend church on any given Sunday, and few churches are making systematic attempts to go out to the unchurched population. Other religions are active, with mosques and Hindu temples a familiar feature, supplemented by New Age shops and centres.

There is a massive leisure and entertainment industry, and shorter working hours, but stress and depression are rampant. Lewis Wolpert wrote in 1999 of a 'malignant sadness' which affects more and more people. Wolpert argued that this is due to biological, genetic factors, and thus needs to be treated medicinally. But if so, there is no hard evidence to explain why the problem is currently growing so extensively. It is just as feasible to link the growth of depression to what one church leader described as the 'vanquishing' of religion in Britain.

In many ways it still seems that *a great town is a great evil*! The call for Christian caring and Christian evangelism is no less evident and urgent than it was in 1835 when the London City Mission was founded. Indeed, London in the third millennium presents a challenge greater than ever.

A flexible and fruitful stability

But, at over 160 years of age, can the London City Mission meet that challenge? It is common in our novelty-worshipping culture of today to assume that old equals out-of-date or irrelevant. That may sometimes be true. But it is not the mere passage of time that makes it so. Others like to think that a much loved and revered organisation will automatically carry on and be effective. But mere age will not guarantee this.

The LCM has always been innovative and adventurous, seizing opportunities to minister to the changing situations and needs of London, while retaining its firm and clear commitment to Biblical Christianity. Of course, it has sometimes made mistakes, but these have not diverted it from going forward. Overcoming several major crises along the way, it has learned to combine the experience of past generations with the enthusiasm and vision of today's workers in a flexible and fruitful stability.

In a new millennium clouded by economic uncertainty and overshadowed by terrorism and war, London will need to hear the Christian message in all its radical and unique clarity. The London City Mission's fundamental strategy of proclaiming that message through:

'the same person,
going to the same people,
regularly,
to become their friend,
for Jesus' sake'

remains as valid as it ever was. Any method of evangelism that ignores this personal, persistent approach is in danger of becoming trite and superficial. As it enters the next chapter in its long story, the London City Mission continues to take the good news of Jesus Christ to a sophisticated, multi-cultural, troubled, and spiritually impoverished city.

Postscript

London City Mission
175 Tower Bridge Road
London   19th September 2002

Dear Sir,

Re: Waterloo Mission / Webber Street

I walk past the above premises several times each week. I have become familiar with some of the faces and occasionally exchange greeting with them. That said, once past by they disappear from your thoughts pretty quickly.

However, yesterday morning was rather different. I walked down Webber Street and side stepped one of the regulars who was face down on the ground, semi-conscious with his hand outstretched towards a beer can. People scurried past, often averting their eyes. They do not consider these 'down-and-outs' worthy of any attention or indeed sympathy. Then I noticed a young man descend from the stairs of your mission. Watching, as I had stopped to have a conversation on my mobile phone, I initially assumed he was coming to make this vagrant move on. But no. Instead he crouched beside this forlorn figure and stroked his face with tenderness and apparent affection.

It was a moving and somewhat shameful moment for me. It made me realise that this person on the street was a real person just like me, albeit perhaps less fortunate. I am grateful for that realisation.

I hope that the attached contribution can be used to assist in the good work of the Webber Street mission.

Yours sincerely, …

For further information about the London City Mission,
write to the following address:

London City Mission
175 Tower Bridge Road
London
SE1 2AH

Tel: 020 7407 7585
Fax: 020 7403 6711

Or look at the LCM website:
www.lcm.org.uk

Bibliography

Ackroyd, Peter, *London, the Biography,* 2000 (London: Vintage)

Barclay, Oliver, *Thomas Fowell Buxton and the Liberation of Slaves,* 2001 (York: Wm. Sessions)

Hall, Peter, *Cities in Civilization: Culture, Innovation and Urban Order,* 1998 (Weidenfield and Nicolson)

Heasman, Kathleen *Evangelicals in Action* London: Bles, 1962

Hanks, Geoffrey, *Sixty Great Founders,* 1995 (Tain: Christian Focus Publications)

Inwood, Stephen, *History of London,* 1999 (London: Macmillan) Merriman, Nick (ed.) *The Peopling of London,* Museum of London, London, 1993

Morris R. J. and Roger R., *The Victorian City,* London: Longman, 1993

Porter, Roy, *London, A Social History,* London: Penguin, 1996

Sources from the LCM Archive

Chapter 1: LCM Mag. Oct. 1947, April 1848, July, Aug., Oct. 1849; Annual Report 1850

Chapter 2: *Memoirs of Nasmith,* John Campbell; LCM Mag. Jan. 1836, July 1837

Chapter 3: LCM Mag. Dec. 1839, Jan., Aug. 1847, June, Aug. 1848, Mar. 1949; Annual Report 1848. *Dens of London: Notes and Narrative of Ten Years Ministry,* R. Vanderkiste (1852)

Chapter 4: *Les Écoles en Haillons; These Fifty Years,* John M. Weylland (1884), LCM Mag. July 1848, Nov. 1849, Feb. 1863, Feb. 1884; Annual Report 1850

Chapter 5: *The Providence that Shapes,* John Galt (unpub.); *These Fifty Years,* (1884) John M. Weylland; *Tales of the City,* John Farley; Missionaries' Journals from 1859 and 1910; LCM Mag. for June 1849, Aug. 1868, Apr. 1869

Chapter 6: *My Adventures with the Coalies' Baby,* Walter J. Prentice; *George Gillman's account of his service with the LCM* (unpub.); LCM Mag. May 1847, Jan./Feb. 1859, May 1872, Jan., May 1873, July 1876, Apr. 1891

Chapter 7: *The Rookeries of London,* Thomas Beames; *Pioneer Work in the Great City,* John Hunt; 'The Bitter Cry of Outcast London', Andrew Mearns; *To Seek and to Save,* Joseph Currie; LCM Mag. Nov. 1883, Mar. 1884, Aug. 1887, Sept. 1899, Apr. 1890

Chapter 8: *Henry Lockyer's Journal* (unpub.); LCM Mag., Oct. 1849, Oct. 1859, Mar. 1887, May, July 1904, Nov. 1905

Chapter 9: *The Providence that Shapes*, John Galt (unpub.)

Chapter 10: Paul Chierico's Journal; LCM Mag. Oct. 1851, Dec. 1852, July 1900; Annual Report 1852

Chapter 11: *George Gillman's account of his service with the LCM* (unpub.); *The Providence that Shapes*, John Galt (unpub.); LCM Mag. for June 1848, Mar. 1930; Annual Report 1913; *Reminiscences of E.B., late Missionary in the London City Mission* (unpub.), Edwin Blanchard

Chapter 12: *My Adventures with the Coalies' Baby*, Walter J. Prentice, *The Kentish Mercury*, 1st Aug. 1930; LCM Mag. Nov. 1915, Nov./Dec. 1917, Jan. 1918, Oct. 1927, Feb. 1928; Annual Reports 1915, 1916, 1917

Chapter 13: LCM Mag. Jan. 1921, Sept. 1923, Dec. 1927.

Chapter 14: LCM Mag. Dec. 1868, Mar. 1889, Feb. 1901, Oct. 1936, Mar. 1937, Sept. 1939, Dec. 1941

Chapter 15: LCM Mag. Oct., Dec. 1939, Mar. 1941, May/June 1942, Jan./Feb., Sept./Oct., Nov./Dec. 1944, May/June 1945, Jan./Feb. 1946. Annual Report 1944

Chapter 16: 'Just like the Country'; LCM Mag. Feb. 1904, Sept./Oct. 1943, Mar./Apr. 1949, Jan./Feb. 1950, Sept./Oct. 1955, Nov. 1959, Nov. 1966, Nov./Dec. 1988

Chapter 17: LCM Mag. Jan./Feb. 1962, Dec. 1966; Annual Report 1961

Chapter 18: LCM Mag. Jan./Feb., Sept./Oct. 1971, Sept./Oct. 1972, July/Aug. 1976, July/Aug. 1978

Chapter 19: LCM Mag. Sept. 1949, Jan. 1959, Nov. 1860, Mar. 1861, Mar. 1903, Nov. 1905, Oct. 1916, Nov. 1935, Aug. 1938, Jan./Feb. 1981, Nov./Dec. 1990; Journal of Frederick Barrington Robinson, 1912

Chapter 20: LCM Mag. Mar./Apr. 1993, Mar./Apr. 1997, Sept./Oct. 1998, May/June, Sept./Oct. 1999, Nov./Dec. 2002

Index

257